Acts *of* Love

November 11, 2007

For Carol and Imre, our "on the road again" friends, in hopes you'll want to come North and West again to Saskatchewan (which, it's rumoured, means: place from which no man can fall to death.) Hugs,
Pat

Acts of Love

A MEMOIR

Pat Krause

COTEAU
BOOKS

Edited by Robert Currie.
Book and cover design by Duncan Campbell.
Cover image by Adrian Weinbrecht /Getty Images.

Printed and bound in Canada at Marquis Bookprinting Inc.
This book is printed on recycled paper.

Library and Archives Canada Cataloguing in Publication

Krause, Pat, 1930–
Acts of love : a memoir / Pat Krause.

ISBN 978-1-55050-368-5

1. Krause, Pat, 1930–. 2. Krause, Pat, 1930–Family. 3. Loss (Psychology)
4. Love. 5. Authors, Canadian (English)–
20th century–Biography. 6. Journalists–Canada–Biography.
I. Title.
PS8571.R39Z463 2007   C813'.54   C2007-903661-9

1 2 3 4 5 6 7 8 9 10

COTEAU
BOOKS
2517 Victoria Ave.
Regina, Saskatchewan
Canada   S4P 0T2

AVAILABLE IN CANADA & THE US FROM
Fitzhenry & Whiteside
195 Allstate Parkway
Markham, ON, Canada, L3R 4T8

The publisher gratefully acknowledges the financial assistance of the Saskatchewan Arts Board, the Canada Council for the Arts, the Government of Canada through the Book Publishing Industry Development Program (BPIDP), the Association for the Export of Canadian Books, and the City of Regina Arts Commission, for its publishing program.

For our family and friends with gratitude
for your many acts of love.

Two doves I bring;
One broods all day;
One has a broken wing;
One is the prayer I have no words to say;
One is the song I have no words to sing.

SISTER MARY MADELEVA [1887-1964]
Presentation

How we harden off
prolong the year, keep our heads
above ground, proud indeed

what care we take
to make it through the ever
shorter seasons

JUDITH KRAUSE
Coldframes and Hotbeds

CONTENTS

Acts of Love

Fragments of Fats Waller's tune "Honey Hush" litter my widow's web of memory. A mishmash of threads at various angles and planes crisscrosses the melody and lyrics. It isn't easy to untangle them by myself. I have to try.

It wasn't our song, romantically. It was our song because of an event only Frank's younger brother remembers. One drink too many at family gatherings, and Stan would swear that in 1947, the night Frank started going steady with me again, we borrowed his 78 RPM record of "Honey Hush" to take to a party and broke it.

"We? Include me out." For decades I used to reply like that to his accusation and, as if to prove my father's boast that he'd taught me to whistle like a lark, I would sing the fourth verse so I could imitate Fats Waller's trilling birdlike whistle at the end of the second line, "Oh, how I love you honey hush/My heart is singing like a thrush...."

Then the others would join in for a family singalong.

The kids loved it. Frank and Stan demonstrated their brotherly love by standing shoulder-to-shoulder and doing an off-key duet. For the finale, I whistled a verse solo.

But that was in another life. I couldn't even remember enough of the tune to hum it anymore, when out of the blue the audiotape arrived. There was just that small package without any postage, only my name written on it, and two business envelopes for Frank in the mailbox. That was it.

Queen Victoria propped Prince Albert's clothes on his chair after he died so she could feel he was there. I didn't have to go that far. I felt Frank watching over my shoulder as I opened his letters.

The envelope from the Centre of Agricultural Medicine, Royal University Hospital, Saskatoon, was full of graphs, stats, a 6-page questionnaire and a form letter thanking Frank for his continued participation in their five-year survey of the long-term health effects of common urban pesticides. *Deadly*, I heard Frank think as I flipped through the pages, *and that's my final answer*.

The Hospitals of Regina Foundation envelope – addressed to *Rev.* instead of *Mr.* – enclosed an appeal for a "generous" donation. I decided to send them a generous number of reasons why, in the wellness age of closed hospital beds and do-it-yourself medical care, my husband chose to die at home twenty-two months ago.

The package was the right size to contain another copy of C.S. Lewis's paperback journal, *A Grief Observed*.

I hadn't ordered a new copy nor hinted to my friends or family that I needed one, but mine was getting messy. On one of its dog-eared pages, Lewis describes the absence of his deceased lover: "Her absence is like the sky, spread over everything." I've changed *absence* to *presence* and in the margin printed the award-winning Saskatchewan license plate slogan: LAND OF LIVING SKIES.

Finding a tape inside the package was a big surprise.

Wrapped around the cassette, a handwritten note from Stan said it was the copy of "Honey Hush" he'd promised to make me if he received a good recording. One came from a man in Kingston, New York, who'd enjoyed being stationed in Canada in WWII when he was in the US armed forces. He'd taken the song off his master recording of a NYC live performance of Fats Waller playing and singing his stride piano compositions, and apologized for taking so long to answer the ad in the Winter '95 issue of *The Good Old Days*.

I opened the cassette case and stared at "Time: 3:07" neatly printed on the tape's label. An ad in *The Good Old Days* magazine Stan subscribes to? The one he loaned Frank with sticky notes on the pages reminiscing about old cars and trucks? A final arrangement I didn't have a clue my old high school sweetheart and his brother were making? Does Frank want me to listen to three minutes and seven seconds of music all alone and then unravel fifty years of memories we made together? Say *mea culpa* to Stan for something we didn't do?

If I concentrate, can I summon Frank back to give me some answers? Hang onto him until he does? While he was dictating his obituary to me, he paused, smiled, and said, "When I return after I'm gone, please detain me so I'll be here when I get back."

Sometimes, when I awake under the 4 a.m. avalanche of sadness, he reaches across my shoulder and places his hand on my face. I stay curled on my side of the bed, my back to his empty pillow, hoping that when I tell him I love him so much it hurts, he'll reply, "Love you too, hon."

But he's silent. A warm presence. He doesn't speak or give advice.

So where to begin? Another decision to make on my own. I'm sixty-six years old and this is the first time in my life I've lived alone. I can't believe how much trouble I am to look after. Busy, busy, busy. So much to do. Accept every invitation. Be cheerful. Keep the corners of my mouth turned up. Nobody likes to see a black widow with an hourglass frown tattooed on her forehead. Half a couple has double the chores. So very much to do. Smile till my cheeks ache. Shop for groceries systematically the way he showed me he did and bring home a seasonal flowering plant to surprise myself. Gas the car, go to the liquor store, pay the household bills, run my own errands, load the dishwasher, vacuum, put out the garbage and Blue Box. Use the old soup pot to carry eight loads of salt crystals from the 20-kilo bag in the trunk of the car down the basement to fill the water softener. Climb the aluminum stepladder with no one to hold it steady to change a smoke alarm battery or to try and twist the ends of fluorescent light tubes into slots I can't see looking up wearing bifocals.

Cope as each change of season adds another partition between then and now. Follow his outdoor work schedule.

Sweep the gravel off the driveway, hook-up the hose, take the tarp off the air conditioner, cut the grass, rake the leaves, put the tarp back on again, wash the furnace filters, reset the outdoor light timers for longer nights, rummage through the stuff in the shed for the plastic snow shovel – done today, just in time.

It's Saturday, October 19, 1996, almost midnight, and a heavy wet snow is falling. I light a 3-hour log in the fireplace. Play the tape. Listen to Fats Waller whisper, "Honey hush," after his final riff on the piano, hug myself, and make up my mind where to start.

These three excerpts from the research I've done about widowhood and Waller fit together best to set the mood.

In his memoir about embalming his undertaker father, "A Death In The Family" in the December 1995 *Harper's* magazine, poet and Michigan undertaker Thomas Lynch recalls that his father, director of the family funeral home, understood that: "The meaning of life is connected, inextricably, to the meaning of death; mourning is a romance in reverse, and if you love, you grieve, and there are no exceptions."

A reverse romance?

Webster Dictionary: romance, Mus. a short, simple melody, vocal or instrumental, of tender character.

"He could make a song and the piano couple in the act of love," biographer Joel Vance says in *Fats Waller: His Life And Times*.

Metal strings struck by felt-covered hammers coupled with tender words. And me, alone, remembering what?

That my light-hearted efforts to flick Stan's stuck needle forward with family songfests didn't work forever? That we exchanged snide remarks over a broken record?

It took Stan three decades to recall that Frank and I borrowed his record to take to a dance on the Ides of March. He claimed it was a Saturday night sock hop on the badminton courts of my hoity-toity Wascana Winter Club where I'd won a silver cup bashing birds around.

"Shuttlecocks!" I said, emphasizing the last syllable. I didn't need to check my diary to know he was wrong. Just me and my shadow were going steady until the day after the Ides of March. It was *Sunday* night, March 16, when my prayers were answered and his big brother came back into my life to stay.

After that, Stan only had to look morosely into his refilled glass and swirl the ice cubes around with his finger to trigger my solo of Fats Waller's "Your Feets Too Big" while I did the jitter-bug waltz out of earshot.

All of our sporadic attempts to find Stan another 78 failed. The sixties phone calls to Library Information Services to ask who'd recorded it – Victor or Bluebird? RCA or Bulldog? – only established that "Honey Hush" wasn't listed in their Fats Waller discographies. Several letters to CBC Radio's Clyde Gilmour in the Seventies and Eighties weren't answered. Searches of vintage vinyl stores in the early Nineties turned up some of his Hit Parade tunes, but it wasn't on the flip side of "Honeysuckle Rose" or "Ain't Misbehavin'" or "Jitterbug Waltz."

Now, here it is. "Honey Hush." A single. On tape. My good old days theme for reverse romance? Not just one more commercial sympathy card message that says – oh, so pitifully rhymed and expressed I can dash one off myself – *May memories most dear / appear in every tear / to keep your loved one near.*

Forget it. Ask any widow. *Memories are history. Kisses of the passed in the past,* I hear Frank whisper. Mirages. Puddles on the road ahead that are tears still unshed. Where's the damn magic?

I punch the rewind button on the Sony and Fats Waller appears, large as life, in the archway at the far end of the living room. I almost fall off the loveseat.

Fats Waller? In person?

He wriggles his caterpillar eyebrows, shines his big spotlight eyes on me, and repeats the only line he had in the 1943 movie, *Stormy Weather,* "One never knows, do one?"

Oh, yes I do. It's him. I saw that movie when I was thirteen, an indelible age, and recorded it in my diary.

Saturday, December 18, 1943: A gang of us went to see Lena Horne in Stormy Weather. *Went to The Winter Club after and talked about life instead of playing badminton. Everybody said it really felt strange to see Fats Waller jazzing it up on the screen when we'd heard on the radio he died three days ago at age thirty-nine. I got a decent quip in, for once. "Too old to live fast, die young, and have a good-looking corpse," I said, "one never knows, do one?" It got a good laugh.*

This week, I borrowed a video of the movie from the library and watched it again. It's an old-fashioned musical loosely based on the story of Bojangles Robinson. There's hardly any dialogue. The first time Fats Waller delivers that one-liner it's one of a string of ad libs he was famous for making while he played a blues or jazz number he found less than inspiring. A female singer is belting out the lyrics of "That Ain't Right" and he's responding as if he's the no-good man she's berating. In his only scene away from a piano, he pauses at the open door of Lena Horne's dressing room, looks down at the rival dancer Bojangles has just laid out with a punch, and says it again.

On December 15, 1943, on a train going to another gig, he died of pneumonia somewhere near Kansas City, Missouri, and I think of the line as his epitaph.

Fats Waller is dead. Long gone to the great beyond. I'm not on the Hollywood set of a crowded Beale Street bistro in an old black-and-white movie. He's not standing there waiting for me to invite him into my living room.

"Baby, baby, say what you sees. Lay on no lies or prefabrications, sweet woman, shoot me the truth," this figment of too much research says.

The truth is, I'm hallucinating and the wrong man has joined me tonight. That's not right.

"Beef to me, mamma, beef to me, I don't like pork nohow." Fats does one of his eyeball rolls.

Frank had a trick like that he did with his eyes. It was a hit in high school. He closed one eye, rolled the other eye up, said it was glass, and pretended to pluck it out. Gruesome was his game. Girls got hysterical, squirmed and squealed, covered their eyes and loved it.

Everyone called him Eyeball, later shortened to Eye. When Stan started grade nine two years behind Frank, he was stuck with the nickname Eye Junior. Beside the grade twelve photo of Frank in Ye *Flame 1945*, our high school yearbook, it says: A *sport. The Eye is our foremost author of topical and horror shorts. Donned blades for this year's ice squad. Curly will likely major in hairdressing.*

For me, Frank's eyeball rolls were love signals, before and after. I smile.

The ad lib maestro winks a fringed-awning eyelid at me. Then he ambles over to the floor-to-ceiling bookcase, sits down on a nonexistent piano stool, pokes his butt, and says, "You all on there, Fats? Yes, sees you is."

That's what he did on opening night at the London Palladium in 1938. His manager was worried about his hangover from alcohol, not what hung over the stool.

He wags his head. Says, "Suffer, excess baggage, suffer." Tips back his hat. Flexes his fingers, runs them back and forth across a shelf of Saskatchewan prose and poetry, and begins to play "Honey Hush."

The spines of the books sing like birds at sunrise. Sweet as summer. Notes flutter. Kiss my ears lightly. Tinkling trills, plaintive burbles, buoyant warbles, soft, tender, the melodies tumbling together exuberantly. It's magic.

I hear the melody Fats Waller heard after a night of insomnia and woke his manager Ed Kirkeby at dawn to help him write.

According to Vance's biography, the spiel Fats used to get him out of bed was, "I was just walking around in the park and the birds were singing so pretty they sang me a tune and I want to get it down on paper before it does like a bird and flies away on me."

I watch as his right hand plays the melody and his left delivers the rhythm. See his fingers fly. Recognize stride piano. The successor to ragtime. Jazz, blues and torch song, played by a wizard in a derby hat.

I shut my eyes. Carefully, gently, not too fast, I press the last images of us together in my mind again.

Frank's sitting up on his side of the bed, his swollen feet on the floor, puffed fingers holding his penis to pee. I'm kneeling beside him holding the curved plastic bottle. His head is bent. The curls of his new growth of hair are as soft as snowflakes on my forehead.

We murmur like mourning doves about the level of pain, more morphine, sips of water, the comfort of his pillows, sleeping soundly, sweet dreams, loving each other. I blow softly in his ear. He smiles, remembering the promise he made. It's carved in stone in my diary.

Sunday, March 16, 1947: Old lover boy Eye's back! Maybe "I'm All Dressed Up With A Broken Heart" won't be my permanent theme song. He says he and the vixen are like two gloves that don't match no matter how often they try. He hinted they'd had a fight and called it quits for good last night. I heard he was her date at a dodge ball court sock hop for R.C. guys only, held by the boy-crazy girls at Sacred Heart Academy, and that nuns measured the distance between dancers with their big crosses turned lengthwise. I said, I know I match you and you match me. He said, Blow in my ear and I'll follow you anywhere. I did. We necked for a while and agreed to go steady again.

"When do you get to sleep?" Frank asks as I get him settled, propped up against the pillows.

I lie down beside him. Listen to him breathe. Stay wide-awake, listening. Match his shallow breaths. Lie perfectly still. Listen. What if?

I gaze up without blinking at the high shelf over our clothes closet where the pair of blue ceramic mourning doves look down on us from their roost. We bought them in Sarasota, Florida, after seeing an accident that deeply affected all four of us in our rental car.

It happened in the late eighties. Frank was driving and my sister Heather's husband, John Verhoeven, was his co-pilot. Heather and I were the designated back-seat drivers. Men in the front and women in the back was a Fifties and Sixties custom we hadn't broken. Heather and John had just arrived from their home in Toronto to spend the last two weeks of April with us and, as usual, the first thing they wanted to do was drive out to Cady's Grove to buy freshly picked grapefruit. In those days, the last few miles to 4975 Clark Road was on a single-lane country road without shoulders.

We were on our way back, almost to the double-lane highway, when John warned Frank to look out for the pair of doves making love on our side of the road. Frank honked the horn as he steered to the middle of the road, and said even a coo-coo bird-brain knows it's dangerous doing it on a roadbed. Heather and I began a duet of the risqué song I'd taught her when she was four and I was fourteen.

The banter ended when we got closer. One of the doves was trying desperately to pull its wounded mate off the side of the road into the ditch. Frank pumped the brake pedal, switched on the flashing emergency lights, and swung from the middle of the road to the other side.

There wasn't any oncoming traffic, but there was a car behind us. We pressed the levers to roll down our windows, made frantic motions with our hands, and yelled, "Swerve-swerve-swerve," at the coiffure of mauve-tinted curls barely visible above the steering wheel of the creeping black Lincoln.

The stupid woman hit them. She was going about fifteen miles an hour. But swallowed up in that black Gastropod slug of hers, she ran over both of them.

The sharp edge of solace seeing them killed together was breathtaking. One bird didn't watch its mate die.

But, as Jesse Jackson said on TV, "Life is uncertain, death is certain."

I have to stay alert. Awake. Listen.

I lie on my left side and watch Frank's chest rise and fall a little as he takes shallow breaths through his open mouth into his fluid-congested lungs. Unlike the cancer, pneumonia is his friend. Frank knows that.

At 4 a.m., Frank suddenly sits bolt upright without my help and moves his legs stiffly over the side of the bed.

"Hey, what're you doing?" I ask softly.

He says he's going down to the kitchen for a soft drink and tries to stand.

Wait-wait, I cry as I'm running around the end of the bed to hold the plastic glass and the oversized bendable straw so he can sip some Gatorade.

I'm there, picking up the glass on his bedside table, and he falls back across the bed in slow motion. Rolls his eyes one last time. Stops breathing. We are both motionless for a long time. I don't know how long. He left orders in his living will not to resuscitate.

I've never seen anyone die before. I hold him. Kiss his closed eyelids and his dry lips. Whisper in his ear I'll love him forever and a day. Remove the oxygen tubes from his nose. Leave him briefly, to switch off the tank. Lift his legs back up on the bed. Turn and lift him so his head is on the pillows again.

Tonight, I let myself circle around the lingering sounds of the Gregorian chant and hissing oxygen tank. Breathe deeply and replace the hospital smell of medicine and formaldehyde with the scent of the blueberry candles on the dresser. Hear Frank say, "We both look nice in blue," after we've put on our new emergency pyjamas. Feel his hand lift my chin and his moist lips against mine.

I suspend the scenes in one of those lacy nets of concentric ladders orb weavers spin.

And I listen as Fats plays and sings "Honey Hush."

Hear each note and word. Shyly, lip-sync the lyrics I knew off by heart half a century ago and didn't really forget. Sing aloud.

Harmonize. Bebop a little bit – shades of Ella. Swing my hips.

Smile when Fats says, "Must be jelly, 'cause jam don't shake like that."

Do a mellow songbird whistle solo. Glide smoothly with Fats into the last verse.

Our voices soar.

"Your eyes shine like stars up above / making me know that I'm in love / Oh my sweet, don't do this to me / tell me you'll be, always with me."

I whisper, "Honey hush."

And slowly dance backwards.

Licence To Live

The two most important men in my life, my husband and my father, both loved cars. They believed being able to drive was a licence to live. So did I. It's a family legend that I became certifiably car-crazy in high school.

Learning to drive took over my life. Sleeping in Saturday mornings even lost its importance – once I'd been fully awakened.

Dad would do his special two-note wake-up whistle, knock on my bedroom door, and call, "Come on, young lady, rise and shine. I've got an hour before hospital rounds. Let's take the car out on the prairie and you can practice shifting gears."

He was quieter than the clangour of my alarm clock on school days, but he couldn't be turned off and reset for later. "Young lady?" He whistled. "Pat?" He rapped. "PAT BLAIR!"

The burst of my name woke me. The jingle of keys made me bounce out of bed and open my door.

Dad would be standing there like a man of distinction pictured in his *Esquire* or *Fortune* magazine, dangling the car keys as if they were for a new Cadillac. His curly white cowlick would be tamed by brushing, his face freshly shaved, moustache trimmed.

He'd be dressed in a Saturday outfit such as his white cable-stitch sweater over a blue plaid shirt, grey trousers, and crepe-soled loafers mirror-polished.

I thought he looked quite sporty and modern for a father who was born in 1900, before cars had been invented.

The car keys he jingled were for our 1937 Chevrolet sedan. We called it the Green Hornet because of its colour and my brother said the motor buzzed like the theme music of *The Green Hornet*, his favourite radio show. Dad bought the Green Hornet in 1937 when we lived in Toronto, and he took pride in keeping it groomed and tuned-up even after it became a home front casualty when I was in grade eight at Lakeview School.

On a Sunday morning in March 1943, when Mother was getting a drink of water before we went to church, she looked out the west window over the sink, and said, "That's funny, there's a green car out there on the prairie that looks like ours." Just then, Dad opened the back door and yelled, "The car's gone."

"Buzzed off," Kenny said, and hummed "Flight of the Bumblebee."

What we found out on the prairie was a dismembered and gutted Green Hornet. Its tires, wheels, headlights, hood ornament, tail light, and everything in the trunk had been stolen. Inside, the roof fabric was ripped, the seats were slashed in several places, the rear-view mirror was gone. So were the glove compartment door, Dad's gas-ration coupons and his liquor permit. Even the gearshift knob that got slippery with sweat from my hand during driving lessons was missing.

The police investigation was futile. They didn't bother to dust the car for fingerprints. They did question the whole family, except three-year-old Heather, about "known enemies," insinuating the vandalism was a personal act of revenge. One policeman grilled me about my boyfriends until I finally admitted I didn't have any boyfriends at all, neither ex nor current. They left saying Dad would be called to identify any parts that turned up on the black market.

Dad added his name to the waiting list at Regina Chevrolet Sales to buy a new car after we'd won the war, and he arranged for the Green Hornet to be made roadworthy again until then.

The trunk latch was quickly fixed so the lid didn't pop up. And, in what Dad called "a stroke of luck," he and Kenny were hitting golf balls near the crime scene when they spied the gearshift knob beside a gopher hole. Finding wheels and good tires in the depot salvage heaps took much longer.

"Not good as new, but it'll do until..." Dad smiled, raised his hand, and made the V-for-Victory sign.

Dad stayed calm about my problems with the clutch. I didn't. Shifting gears made my hands sweat because doing it smoothly was all in the footwork, just like dancing. Learning to stop and start had been easy. Steering, speeding in high gear along the ruts in the prairie trails beyond our house, quick turns, were so simple they must have been inherited skills. What gave me trouble was getting into high gear without neck-snapping jerks.

"Practice," my father would say as we got into the car. "What you need is practice in foot control and coordination."

Maybe instead of a doctor he should have been a dance instructor. I couldn't get the right rhythm to jitterbug either. At the Saturday afternoon Junior Assembly dance classes at

Government House in grade eight, all I learned was not to count foxtrot steps aloud and to be ultra-polite to my so-called "young gentlemen" partners who stomped on my feet, but whose lead I was expected to follow. I was too self-conscious to practise dancing with the girls at slumber parties. I minded the record player. I went to the free Saturday afternoon jive sessions for teenagers that were held in Regina City Hall auditorium and watched from the balcony.

Maybe I wasn't much of a dancer, but beat-me-daddy-eight-to-the-bar, I was going to learn to drive or die trying.

I practised dancing the Shift Stick Shuffle before bed each night. I would sit at my desk with my right foot on the gas, lift my left foot and press it firmly on my algebra text until I could feel the binding give, and then, raising my left foot slowly, I would shift my pen from low into intermediate on my blotter. A little more gas, repeat the routine, and I'd have my desk in high gear without a single buck or grind. Practising wasn't a waste of time because I showed improvement.

"Fine," Dad said. "That's smoother. Now next time, let the clutch up even slower and it won't jerk at all."

I made a perfect stop; clutch to the floor, brake, shift to low, brake gently to a stop, and turn off the key. I started the car again like an expert; clutch right to the floor, turn on key, press starter, check that gear's in low, press gas pedal and release clutch slowly. Now, intermediate; clutch down, up slowly after the gear goes through neutral and into second. "Jeez!" I said, "I've got it." And high, clutch down, shift down to the right, and clutch up. "Jeez," I yelled, "this is great."

"Great driving, bad use of the language," Dad said. "Vulgar slang causes cankers. You can expect two on your tongue, young lady, one for each use of a slang nickname for Jesus that's too close for comfort to blasphemous. In extreme moments of stress, damn, said gently, would be more ladylike."

"Damn-damn, I'm a ladylike driver," I cried. I pushed the gas pedal to the floor and we careened across the prairie, both laughing raucously.

I wondered what Perkins would do if I tried a few ladylike damns in his algebra class. Probably throw the chalk at me again, and a hundred percent in the final exam wouldn't save me from extinction. I honked the horn. Jeez-damn, this was great.

But Dad wasn't fooling about his ideas of what was ladylike and what wasn't. He had a prescription for bringing me up a "well-rounded young lady."

It included alcohol in minute quantities. "Well-rounded young ladies know how to handle alcoholic drinks," he said. "Take a small drink and sip it – make it last. There's nothing sloppier than a tipsy woman. Her bobby pins fall out, her silk stockings sag, and she'll either start giggling or weeping."

He offered me a thimbleful of sherry on Sundays before dinner. It sure wasn't enough to gear my laugh down to a giggle, but I had to discreetly hide my unladylike gagging.

Dad's prescription didn't include cigarettes. "People who smoke, spit," he said, although he smoked and I'd never seen him spit. "Well-rounded young ladies do neither."

Everyone else knew that cigarette skill was a social grace worth having. Daph and I first tried smoking down in our furnace room using Dad's Player's Plain butts held in bobby pins. Since then, I'd shared a cigarette with Central girls in the ladies' washroom at The Glasgow House department store and in the locker rooms of the Winter Club and Tennis Club. Lighting up a weed in the Edgewater at the northwest end of Albert Street Bridge, or in Scotty's Tearoom kitty-corner from Central, meant you were one of the in-crowd.

The best part of Dad's prescription was, "A well-rounded young lady is a good driver." Learning to drive would change my whole personality. Cure the rare African laughing disease I'd caught reading his medical books, the one that made me snort. I'd become a Big Wheel. Know what to say to guys. Telling dreamboats I already had a date for the dance or movie without hurting their feelings would become a habit. When I tooled up to the Edgewater in the Green Hornet, I'd be swamped in dreamboats. Greek gods would be clamouring to go for a ride with me, flirt with me, date me. My diary would sizzle. I just had to pass Dad's driving tests and wait to be sweet sixteen, pay two dollars, and sign my licence to live. Jeez, by January 26, 1946, I'd be a junior in grade eleven.

I added an urgent request to my nightly Lord's Prayer. After "Deliver me from evil," I prayed: "And please grant me patience immediately."

Every driving lesson included several variations of Dad's Damn Fool lecture: "The most important thing to remember is that every car on the road has a damn fool behind the wheel. Keep your wits about you. Watch for fools everywhere. Look in the rear-view mirror. A damn fool at every wheel, don't forget it."

I would look alert and swerve smoothly, pretending other cars were on the empty prairie, damn fools behind their wheels.

One Saturday morning my lesson had to be delayed because all of our gas had been siphoned. This time, the motor wouldn't catch even when I used the choke. Why didn't those creeps siphon it dry on Saturday nights and we'd only have to skip church? Why didn't Dad camouflage the licence plate? His one-dash licence plate advertised it was a doctor's car and its owner got extra gas ration coupons. And why was it so often parked beside our house instead of in the garage where it belonged? Stupid. Really stupid to let it sit outside on the edge of the prairie with no neighbours or street lights within a block. It was an invitation to vampires to suck the life's blood from the Green Hornet and me. Jeez, those hose-suckers usually left enough gas in the tank for us to drive to the service station.

"Damn it," Dad said when the motor didn't even cough. "Not a drop left to start it, greedy kids. Bad manners. Well, it's a beautiful day. Come on, young lady, let's walk to the service station. Exercise is good for a girl's complexion."

I went, but damn it, I hadn't got up for my complexion. Reg Carter's B/A Service Station was across the bridge and away up Albert on Fifteenth Avenue. By the time we'd walked there and back with gas, my driving lesson would have to be cancelled.

Dad made a heroic effort to lift my gloom. He talked while we walked, mostly about what I liked best about my second year at Central and what he remembered was the "cat's meow" during his four years there. He'd graduated in 1917 at age seventeen, the age I was going to be when I graduated in 1947. He'd convinced me I would love taking Latin as much as he had because it was the origin of the Romance languages, and asked how I was doing learning declensions.

"Veni, Vidi, Vici," I replied.

He laughed, patted my shoulder, and said, "Alite flammam," which everybody knew – even if they didn't take Latin – was the Central motto: Keep the flame lighted or burning.

I didn't tell him I'd skipped Latin, gotten caught, and in the Detention Room I'd locked eyes with a dreamy guy nicknamed Eyeball. Or confess that when I was dreaming *amour gignit amorem*, Eyeball winked at me as if he was also thinking and hoping *love begets love*. Dad would be interested to know Eyeball was a really Big Wheel at Central because he bought and fixed old cars to drive and didn't just wheel around town in his father's car. But my heart beat faster just thinking about Eyeball.

Dad said, "Looks like my prognosis for your complexion was right, judging from its rosy glow."

On the first Saturday of April, Dad said, "You've conquered the imaginary fools on the prairie trails so let's head the other way, toward downtown. April Fool's Day is an excellent opportunity to test your reactions to the ones on the road."

I patted the Green Hornet on the dash and the dance began: clutch, key, starter, gear, gas – we were away, a perfect pair. We did a swirling, ditch-to-ditch U-turn without so much as grazing the water standpipe on our corner – although it was close and my father leaned away from his door. We aimed ourselves north on Robinson Street. I was the leading partner, but the Hornet didn't miss a beat. We had perfect rhythm. I slowed down as we passed the house of a Central dreamboat nicknamed Satch. He was sitting on his front steps when I walked by to high school my first day, and he called, "Hey Butterball, don't break the wooden sidewalk marching off to boot camp." He wasn't there, but I honked the horn. Who says I don't have the footwork to dance? My saddle shoe was smack flat on the floor.

The back of the Hornet slewed around a bit as we waltzed onto the pavement on McCallum Avenue. "Ease up," Dad said. "There's a stop sign at Albert and that means *full stop*."

The instant he said "full stop" I hit the brakes. Dad's head hit the windshield with a *thunk*. That flustered me. I shifted gears, revved the motor, and jeez – reverse? Back we shot – *thunk*. "Hell's bells!" Dad yelled, and I panicked and hit the brakes again – *thunk!* "Judas Priest!" Silence. Dad and the motor had stalled in unison.

"Ohh..." Dad groaned, "concussion – cripes, and my tongue."

I opened my mouth. Diagnose cankers caused by slang? No. Blaspheme? Cripes no. Jeez cripes, no. I shut my mouth and bit my bottom lip.

I fumbled around and got the car started again, made an illegal U-turn, after checking that my father's eyes were still closed, and headed home. Slowly. It took a lifetime.

Dad didn't wait for the car to come to a full stop. He bailed out and went into the house with his hand on his forehead. I sat slumped over the steering wheel and pounded the dashboard with my fists. Damn Green Hornet. Old junk heap ought to be on a scrap pile. I scratched a line down the driver's side with the keys after I got out. Then I did the stumblebum shuffle into the house, dropped the keys on the buffet, and went for a walk on the prairie.

My chance to solo came unexpectedly. Dr. and Mrs. Shaw were coming from Toronto for a visit the last weekend in April. My parents were delighted they were finally going to see the West and made plans to take them on a tour of the Qu'Appelle Valley on Saturday. I heard Dad arranging to borrow a better car for the trip. He promised to take Heather and Kenny. Perfect. I didn't have to babysit. I planned to ask Dad to leave me the keys for the Green Hornet.

House guests and cocktail parties always relaxed the rules a bit, but they didn't erase them. I stayed out past my curfew on Friday night and Dad wasn't happy about it. It wasn't a good time to ask. I decided to wait until morning.

I slept until almost noon. Didn't even hear them leave. Stupid. Really stupid. Why didn't anyone wake me up? How come I wasn't asked to go along? Maybe I could have been coaxed into it. I drooped around the empty house feeling invisible. And then, jeez, there they were. The keys. Was I dreaming? No. They were there, right on the front of the buffet. Glistening like jewels on the silver tray. The keys for what it was rumoured Central's Big Wheels referred to as "Doc B's Chevy gas pump." A new life for the Green Hornet and me – the key ring was a wedding band on my finger. What a great Dad. I hadn't even asked. Jeez. I'd wasted hours sleeping. Who should I phone first? It had to be someone reliable who would phone the others to get ready because the driver didn't bother with things like that.

I used the ignition key to dial Daph's number: 6950.

"Hi, Daph? Yeah, Pat. I just got up too." I yawned and tried to sound bored. "Dad left me the car for the day. You busy? Need a ride anywhere? Jeez, I dunno, nowhere special, just tool around town I guess." Daph agreed to phone a couple of our best friends. I picked Daph up first and then the others. I just honked the horn at each house. Cigarettes were lit and we tooled all through downtown Regina.

Kids were lined up for the matinee at the Cap. We waved our weeds at them every time we passed. Dad's lessons had really paid off. Anyone could see I was an experienced driver – comfortable behind the wheel, talking, laughing, smoking – I just let the cigarette hang from my mouth when I shifted gears. We parked quite a few times at the Edgewater. I didn't shut the motor off. A few guys, not really Big Wheels but not drips, came out to the car and kibitzed around each time. I rested my arm on the window frame, elbow poked out, my hand lightly on the wheel, exhaling cigarette smoke out my nostrils.

I figured I should have the Green Hornet home by five o'clock, parked in the same spot beside the house. Smoke cleared out. Keys back on the buffet. I would thank Dad while they were all sipping cocktails. He would get that great-going-young-lady look on his face. His moustache would twitch as he held back a proud smile. He'd be interested to hear I'd slid through the gears as smoothly and silently as he did.

By twenty to five I'd dropped everyone off at home except Daph. "What about tooling by the Edgewater once more?" I suggested. "Do one more detour over Retallack Street Bridge and down Nineteenth to Albert?"

Daph looked at her watch. "Okay," she said, "but we can't stop long; I've got a date with Atlas tonight."

"With Atlas?"

"Look out!" Daph yelled.

I yanked the wheel to avoid ploughing into the lilac bushes at Angus Boulevard. "Are you going steady?"

"Guess so, at least until after the Central election. My brother's his campaign manager and I'm his assistant in charge of publicity – posters, parade, cheers and stuff."

"He'll win Athletics for sure," I said.

"He'd better," Daph said. "Otherwise he's gone. He keeps threatening to lie about his age and join the RCAF. Says if he doesn't do it soon the war will be over and he'll miss his chance to get free flying lessons."

I pulled up to the stop sign about ten feet from the Edgewater. We turned our heads to see who was at the counter through the row of windows facing the bridge.

"Wouldn't you know it?" I took a long drag and exhaled as slowly as a sigh. "All the Big Wheels are in there now. Isn't that Eyeball with those guys and glam-gals?"

"Yeah, but we've gotta go," Daph said.

I shifted gears with the last cigarette of my solo day dangling from my lips, looked both ways, north up Albert for vehicles and people, south down the bridge sidewalk for pedestrians – Lesson Number 6. No traffic, except in the Edgewater. I glanced back for one more look. Some damn fool in an old Studebaker sped up behind me, screeched to a stop at the Hornet's bumper, and honked. I pulled out onto Albert with a lurch and, jeez, what a shock – a dusty black Ford doing a hundred miles an hour was aimed right at us.

I slammed the clutch to the floor, ground the gears through second to high, jammed the wheel right, and went halfway across the bridge with the two right tires scraping the curb. But what caused me to flip the lit end of my cigarette up my nostril and screech to a stop in the middle of the world's longest bridge over the smallest body of water was the voice I heard as the Ford swerved to miss us: "That DAMN FOOL! Right out into the traffic without – my GOD! It's my *daughter.*"

My father parked the borrowed car ahead of me, walked back

to the driver's side of the Green Hornet, and told me to get the car home "fast" – speedily corrected to "slowly and carefully."
I wasn't able to sneak by the living room upstairs to my bedroom. My father's lecture was based on his motto for the cancer clinic. He said, "Errors of omission are inexcusable, and you didn't ask permission to take the car. Errors of commission are regarded with tolerance and understanding. I left the keys in plain sight, you lurched out from a stop sign, but I'm proud that your skill and our teamwork swerving averted a collision."
Mother and Dr. and Mrs. Shaw smiled and nodded.
My father cleared his throat. "Of course, that doesn't change the fact that looking at oneself in a smoky car's rear-view mirror will reveal there's a damn fool behind the wheel." He didn't smile, but his moustache twitched.
The others laughed. I suddenly realized that maybe my father's lecture and his smoke-and-mirror joke showed he liked me.

I didn't attempt to record the mortifying scenes that followed in my diary: my father's bad joke about spitting not being the only danger involved in smoking, the pain of a laughing and snorting seizure I couldn't stop, the snot-yellow Ozonol salve that Dad and Dr. Shaw made me force up my burnt nostril so I couldn't blow it out and get rid of its sheepish smell.
I simply wrote:
Dear Diary: I won't get around much anymore. I'll never get to drive my dad's car. None of the Big Wheels in Central are going to remember me. The only remarkable thing I'm going to do is get through to the end of June as the unknown freshie with the scab on her right nostril, the one who walks alone.

Webs

It's early May, 1932, one of those hot humid mornings in Tuscaloosa that are sticky as glue, and my father is all dressed up in his new blue and white pinstriped seersucker suit. Lily tucks an hibiscus blossom in his lapel buttonhole, a bright red trumpet, she says, on account of the occasion. He's on his way to the Druid City Hospital to get my mother and new baby brother.

Our front porch is a Welcome Home stage. The kitchen band my father arranged for is tuning up their pots and pans, glasses and jugs. A black man wearing a top hat runs wooden spoons up and down different sized washboards.

I sit on the wicker porch swing right where Lily plunked me and said to stay put or else. I'm not supposed to get a speck of dirt on my Sunday dress. Mother says my Godmother Ormie could have won the Dixieland World Champion Smocking Ribbon for this dress at the Alabama State Fair. It's too small for me now. After Lily helps me out of it, I'll have smock-marks on my chest and around my upper arms. But Lily wants me to look sweet as pecan pie for my brother's homecoming. She says it won't do me a bit of good to fret about my dress being a mite tight.

Lincoln, the man who does the cleaning at my father's lab, is the leader of the band. He tells me that today I look as pretty as Miss Shirley Temple. I twist the only ringlet Lily was able to press into my boy's-bob with my mother's curling iron and ask if he'll please get his band to play the spider song my daddy always whistles. The band members know the words:

> *Itty-bitty spider*
> *up the waterspout.*
> *Down comes a raindrop*
> *to wash the spider out.*
> *Out comes the sunshine*
> *and dries up the rain.*
> *Itty-bitty spider's*
> *up the spout again.*

They harmonize, like everyone does at the revival tent Lily takes me to sometimes when she says she just has to cut loose and let her voice fly up to the Lord. Then they sing it in rounds and I join in.

Lily doesn't sing a note. She thrums the wicker behind my back with her blunt grey fingernails. "Honey chile," she leans over and whispers in my ear, "them nasty spiders gon' get your daddy one day, less you be cautious. You jess askin for trouble singin so sweet bout one."

I shiver and clamp my mouth shut.

I'm afraid of spiders now, dead or alive. Lily knows my secret. She came along with us last summer when we drove up to Canada to stay at my grandmother Wilson's lake cottage.

Everyone said it was the driest year in Saskatchewan history. The uncle who took over the family farm near Indian Head after Grandpa Wilson retired to town kept complaining his wheat wasn't heading out worth a goddamn. My grandmother and mother and Lily killed every spider they could find to bring on rain. Lily was towelling me dry after a swim when the fat brown spider crawled right up to me. I stamped on it. The spider squished under the sole of my rubber bathing shoe like a burnt marshmallow. I jerked my foot up and saw spiderlings race out of the mush toward dark corners of the veranda like tiny red sparks from a dead sun. Lily started to sing "Didn't It Rain," then she saw the look on my face. My uncle cleaned up the mess with his cigarette papers, muttering while he did it about its stench, and if the damn grasshoppers or an early frost didn't wipe him out, my fast footwork stomping a spider so big was sure as hell going to cause a cloudburst that would rust out his bumper crop. I threw up on Lily's lap. She remembers.

When we hear the roadster's horn and the toot-toot replies from other cars over on University Boulevard, Lincoln's band begins to play "My Blue Heaven."

"Men folk an' sons!" Lily says, fluffing up the puffed sleeves of my dress. "Mmmm-mmm. You still the one's daddy's girl."

My father has the baby tucked along one arm like a football and his other arm around my mother's waist as they dance toward us. My mother is wearing the georgette dress she got married in. She keeps it wrapped in tissue paper and only wears it on special occasions. Lily likes to try the dress on and twirl through the house in it when my mother is out. She says its whupped-cream colour and dippy-do hem light as spiderweb on her ankles make her feel uppity as a white lady. Sometimes she gets the matching hat with organdy cabbage roses on its wide floppy brim out of the round hat box at the back of the closet shelf and puts it on too. It's our secret, I promised. She made me spit in my shoe and swear never to tell.

"Hey, l'il booger," Lily greets the baby when my father hands him to her. She cuddles him to her thin body and looks my mother over, head to toe. "Welcome home, m'am," she says. "You lookin mighty fine, Missus B, though that ole dress doan do nothin to accentuate it. It jess doan look good on you no more. No m'am, it sure nough doan."

Mother does a few steps of the Charleston, and the dipping hem swishes around her ankles. "Still fits like a glove, Lily. But it'll be yours when I can part with it," she says. "I promise."

"Hey, Miss Tuscaloo," my father says, scooping me off the swing and setting me on his shoulders. "How do you like your new baby brother? Some handsome little man, isn't he?"

I rest my chin on my father's head and look down at the baby. "Uh-huh," I say. He looks like my Wetums doll. "Daddy, can I go with you to see your spiders again?" I ask. "Just you and me?"

My father's lab is painted cream and green and it smells like a hospital. We scrub our hands at the sink, and my father gives me one of his white lab coats to put on. He rolls up the sleeves for me. I try, but I can't reach the patch pockets to dig my hands down in them like he does.

There are two long shelves of black widow spiders in oblong jars for him to show me. Cards with their histories on them are held upright on the lids. My father has been studying black widow spiders for as long as I can remember: collecting specimens, trying to breed them, taking venom from their poison sacs and injecting it into his lab animals.

"Rats and mice die, just like that," he tells me, snapping his fingers. "My guinea pigs get quite ill, but most survive. Rabbits, cats and dogs aren't seriously affected. I suspect they build up an immunity to the widow's venom."

"Lily says people die if they get bitten."

"No, no they don't, hardly ever. Dr. Bogen studied four hundred cases of documented black widow spider poisoning from 1720 to 1931 and only twelve of the people died."

Twelve! I start counting: Daddy and me and my mother and Lily and my baby brother and my best friend Ann Struthers and godmother Ormie and her son M.T., Grandma Wilson and all our kinfolk in Canada like –

"Not that you want to play around asking to be bitten," my father says. "But a widow's web is easy to recognize. Here's a perfect example. See this?"

I look in the jar he points at.

"See how messy it is? How the threads are all helter-skelter, crisscrossing at various angles and planes?"

"Uh-huh," I say.

"A widow usually builds her web in a crevice or corner. That's so she can retreat in a hurry, sometimes through a poorly formed tunnel of silk, like here." He taps on the glass.

"Oh!" I cry, as the spider darts toward his finger.

My father chuckles, and says, "She's cranky, not used to living in a glass jar yet. Probably thought I was going to steal some of her web. You know why, Miss Tuscaloo? A widow's silk is considered to be of a much finer quality than a silkworm's. If I collected enough of it, maybe I could get a pretty dress made for you out of spider silk."

I don't say anything.

"Black widows spin the silk threads used for cross-sections in telescopic sights. A single strand of it is as strong as a steel wire of equivalent thickness. That's why the wicked widow can weave a death cradle for victims many times her size. See what this vicious little lady has trapped in hers? Lincoln swept a mouse nest out from under the stairs yesterday."

He lifts me up so my eyes are level with a jar on the top shelf. Up near the lid, a tiny pink baby mouse is suspended in a silk shroud. The spider is on the mouse's stomach. I shut my eyes; swallow hard.

"She's been having a feast sucking its juices ever since we dropped it in there. Lincoln didn't think her web would hold it. Don't worry, though, the mouse didn't suffer. That nasty lady's venom is fifteen times deadlier than a rattlesnake's. It's a good thing for us that the amount of poison she can shoot in is a lot less than a rattler's."

EXPERIMENTAL BITE IN MAN

10:45 A.M., Sunday, November 12, 1933

He gently grasps the black widow spider by its abdomen with a pair of splinter forceps and places it on the little finger of his left hand.

The spider bites instantly.

Spider Number 111.33 that he selected for his experiment has not been fed for fifteen days. It is an active healthy specimen that he captured in a rock pile at the edge of the cotton field across from our house on Hackberry Lane. Its bulbous abdomen is half an inch in length and in width at the posterior, glossy black, and has on its underside the characteristic adult female marking of a red hourglass.

The subject of the experiment is age thirty-two, five feet eleven inches in height, weighs 168 pounds (76.2 kg), is athletically inclined and in excellent health. He played quarterback on a winning team at McGill University and has recently won the University of Alabama Faculty of Medicine singles tennis cup. His reaction to bee stings and mosquito bites is normal.

He permits the spider to bite him for ten seconds.

The spider twists its cephalothorax from side to side as though to sink its poison claws deeper into his flesh. Venom is being discharged through the tiny openings near the tip of each claw. He records the sensation as being like the prick of a sharp hot needle, accompanied by a localized burning that increases in intensity during the biting period.

After he removes the spider and replaces it in its jar, a drop of clear fluid, slightly streaked with brown, remains at the site of the bite. He leaves this untouched for one minute before wiping it off with a cotton pledget. No definite marks of skin puncture can be seen with the naked eye or with low magnification.

The lymphatic absorption of the poison takes fifty minutes. He makes detailed notes on how the pain spreads and worsens.

An explosive onset of widespread muscular pains and profound shock occurs as the venom begins to circulate in his bloodstream. Aching pains are present in the muscles of his neck and the pit of his stomach. There is a feeling of general malaise. His blood pressure is 108 systolic and 82 diastolic; his pulse is weak, and its rate is 62.

From this stage on, the two medical students assisting him, Griffith and Porter, take over the record keeping.

There is a flushed trembling feeling in his legs. His speech is jerky, respiration rapid and laboured. Sharp brisk expirations are followed by loud grunts. His pulse is rapid, weak, and too thready to count. The heart sounds are slow, his abdomen rigid, and boardlike.

He asks Griffith and Porter to take him to the Veterans Hospital where he has arranged with Chief of Staff Dr. Herbert Caldwell to admit him for an electrocardiograph if he needs it. During the fifteen minutes it takes to drive him there his abdominal pains become rapidly more severe.

It is torture for him to lie still on his back while two electro-cardiograms are made. They do not show any heart damage, but his skin is cold and clammy, his lips are contracted by pain, caus-ing his mouth to assume an oval shape. At his request, his assis-tants run a hot bath and lower him into it, which, he is able to state, brings him considerable relief from the pain.

Dr. J. M. Forney, the attending physician, first sees him at this stage of the spider poisoning and writes his observations in the record: *I found the patient in excruciating pain, gasping for breath, and reclining in a tub of very warm water. I do not recall having seen more abject pain manifested in any other medical or surgical condition.*

For more than forty-eight hours, the clinical chart of his res-piratory rate, blood pressure and pulse is a series of jagged lines. Uh-huh, he remarks when it's shown to him, the widow's web.

On November 15, three days after the bite and thirteen days before his thirty-third birthday, he has almost completely recovered from the poisoning. Rheumatoid pains in his legs and feet, causing a feeling of shakiness when he stands or walks, are his chief complaints. Dr. Forney agrees with his decision to leave the hospital on condition he goes home by ambulance.

It isn't porch weather for his homecoming. Nobody minds. My brother is in a brushed cotton bunting with a hood that has rabbit ears on it. I'm cosy as a kitten in my Chesapeake Railroad overalls and a heavy pullover sweater my grandmother up in Canada sent me. Lily has my father's Harris Tweed jacket on over her long-sleeved winter uniform. She holds my brother on her hip and I stand beside them at the top of the porch steps. Behind us, the men in Lincoln's kitchen band are keeping warm by taking turns tap dancing up and down the length of the porch.

My mother, who says her thick Saskatchewan blood has gotten thin living in Alabama, is all bundled up in what she calls her "snow angel cloak"–a knitted white angora cape that makes her look as pretty as a butterfly. She's waiting down at the end of the sidewalk with Lincoln and two news reporters.

When we see the ambulance cross McFarland Avenue on the far side of the cotton field, Lincoln holds an egg beater up over his head and spins the blades to signal the band to start playing. They strike up with "Just A Closer Walk With Thee." Lily jiggles my brother on her hip and starts humming, then lets loose with bebop words in finger-snapping rhythm before she sings ringing hallelujahs.

The attendants lift my father out of the ambulance on a stretcher. His hands are clasped behind his head, his legs crossed, and he's fully dressed from his shoes to the red plaid bow tie at the neck of the lab coat he's wearing over his tweed suit. He thanks the attendants for the nice smooth ride he had in the ambulance, gets off the stretcher, shakes their hands, and takes a few shaky soft-shoe steps toward us.

My mother walks on one side of him, holding his hand, Lincoln on the other side, his big black hand splayed on my father's arm like a giant spider. Their smiles are watermelon slices.

The Tuscaloosa News and Associated Press reporters walk backwards toward us, squatting and stretching to take pictures, flashbulbs exploding. The band plays "When The Saints Go Marching In" to match their quickening steps. The old man who blows in the jugs makes them sound like trumpets and bugles. I think our kinfolk must hear Lily singing up in Canada.

My father sits down on one of the plantation rockers. Mother runs inside for a blanket to tuck over his knees. After the band stops playing, the reporters ask questions.

Did he know black widow spider venom is deadlier than a rattlesnake's?

Yes, my father says, in equal amounts it's supposed to be. He knew that. And now he believes it's true. He smiles.

Why take such a risk letting one bite you then, Doctor?

That's what I want to know too, but my brother starts to howl so Lily grabs my arm and hauls me along with her when she takes him into the house.

M other lets me help paste clippings in a scrapbook. She reads the two front-page headlines out loud: "U. of A. Professor Lets Spider Bite Him, Suffers 3 Days Agony" (The

Tuscaloosa News, Thursday, November 16); "Scientific Act by Regina M.D. - Submits To Agonizing Experience in Order to Aid Science" (*The Regina Leader-Post*, Saturday, November 25). I think my daddy found the cure for black widow spider bites.

"Beg pardon, Missus B," Lily says, turning from the sink where she's singeing pinfeathers off a chicken with torches made from discarded parts of the newspapers. "Jes' seem to me he bin askin for agony, foolin with them red-spotted coal black widow ladies, 'stead of devotin his self to y'all, considerin."

"You read my mind, Lily," Mother says. "But this time the foolish fly was lured into the spider's parlour and came out a hero. This clipping says he was braver than the Mississippi convicts who were guinea pigs for the St. Louis physicians trying to find out how sleeping sickness is transmitted."

"Spect men wantin free got reason nough to let their selfs be guinea pigs. Ain't no reason the doctor got to go seekin no glory that way, ask me," Lily says.

"Or me," Mother agrees. "Though I have to say I'm glad he didn't accept my offer to let that spider bite me."

I don't say anything. The Associated Press account of the experiment I'm pasting in the book has lots of pictures of my father and his spiders. Mother says it was chosen as one of the ten best human-interest stories of the year. I can't help thinking it's sort of exciting to have a father who's famous.

But later, my father hears that he won't be getting a research job he wanted because he's too famous.

Too much publicity about his work with red-spotted coal black ladies, he tells my mother, his research should have been published in one of the medical journals first. He says the American Medical Association doesn't approve of doctors who do experiments on themselves; they think it's unscientific, if not downright foolish.

Well, my mother says, well.

My father says he's sick of pathology and never having any patients who can talk back to him. He says he's fed up watching to see if a black widow spider eats her mate.

Good, my mother says, get rid of those damn spiders.

He tells her he loves teaching and learning, but that life is too slow and easy for him in the South, that before long he'll be able to do what he's doing in his sleep and he's afraid he'll get to enjoy that. He says she knows how easily he can be seduced, and then he puts his arms around her and gives her a kiss.

Well, my mother says, now what?

He wants to use the savings they've banked in Canada to go north and study surgery, radiology, learn everything he can about the diagnosis and treatment of cancer – seek a new challenge.

They decide to move home, home to Canada.

Home, my father explains to me, isn't necessarily a person's birthplace. He says my brother and I will always have close ties to Tuscaloosa, to Alabama. Webs spun by the Deep South around her sons and daughters, he says, are even stronger than black widow spider silk.

It's almost midnight Saturday, November 13, 1948. I've come down to the dark corner of our basement with my flashlight to look for my father's black widow spiders in the Tuscaloosa trunk. Underneath the old Alabama clothes my mother has saved, there's a large maroon box full of spiders suspended in glass slides. I discovered them when I was nine years old, soon after we'd moved to Regina. They wait with hooked claws ready to strike, their mouths open to suck my body dry if I make a false move or shift my eyes even a fraction while I dig down into the trunk for them. When I was thirteen, if my parents stayed out late on nights I was left in charge of my brother and three-year-old sister, Heather, I used to lie in my bed too scared to move a muscle, listening and listening, afraid that the spiders had come alive, shattered their glass slides, and were creeping up the stairs to get me. Sometimes I had to force myself to come down here to make sure the spiders were only specimens trapped on *Wratten M Dry Plate* slides and not like the darting spiders my father kept in the jars in his lab.

I shudder.

Sleet pings on the windowpane. The cement floor is an ice floe. I don't care if I get chilblains and pneumonia from being down here in my bare feet and pyjamas. There has to be a reason.

M y father is dead. He was buried in the Indian Head cemetery near Mother's father this afternoon. Hearing the earth fall on his coffin was the worst part: the thud of dirt frozen to rocks. But I didn't cry. I won't cry.

He didn't suffer, my mother says. It was so quick he didn't feel any pain. She keeps repeating this.

I saw my father have his first heart attack. She must have forgotten that. He shouted "Hey," fell down on the rug all hunched up, and writhed around, pounding his chest with his fists, grunting, gasping for breath through a fish-shaped mouth.

By the time the doctor arrived, he was lying on the chester-field, the pain almost gone. They decided he'd had a severe attack of indigestion. A year later he had another attack, far worse, and their diagnosis changed.

The three-month recuperation after his third heart attack was almost over. He was back at the cancer clinic part-time.

A soft wet snow fell on his last morning. He and Mother stood for a long time at the kitchen window admiring the way the prairie grass looked with puffs of snow on it. He said it would be easy to mistake the prairie for a cotton field ready for picking. Mother says he was whistling the spider song when he went upstairs after lunch for the prescribed nap he hated taking.

Mother had just started doing the dishes when he called her name. She ran up to their bedroom, the sopping wet dishrag still clutched in her hand. There's a white mark on the bedside table where she dropped it.

He looked as if he'd fallen asleep just as something surprised him, Mother says, there was a startled look on his face and his mouth was open as if he'd just exclaimed, "Oh!" She gave him mouth-to-mouth resuscitation, phoned the doctor, the ambu-lance, and a close friend who was a nurse.

There was nothing anyone could do. It was too late.

Fifteen years too late? A newspaper article said his premature death could have resulted from cardiac damage caused when he allowed a black widow spider to bite him to test the effects of its venom on the human heart.

"No!" Mother shouted when she read it. "Won't those damn spiders ever be forgotten?" She crumpled the newspaper page and hurled it across the living room. "That's not why he let that spider bite him. It's not!"

"Why did he?" I asked her. "Why?" I wanted to scream questions at her. Was it true she'd volunteered to let the spider bite her and he'd refused her offer? Isn't that what she'd told Lily when I was pasting articles in the scrapbook? Did he want to let it bite him to show how brave he was? Did you want him to do it so he'd be a hero? Didn't he care if he died? Did he love those spiders more than us?

"He wanted to know how to diagnose and treat black widow spider poisoning. He thought one bite might give him immunity to others. But he said he didn't have the courage to finish the experiment by being bitten again to prove it. Courage?" Mother looked at me. "Well, maybe it was. But it was foolish, too. There was something so damn seductive about those bloody little coal black widows."

We stared at each other. I had sometimes boasted to my friends that my father was the famous scientist who had discovered a cure for black widow spider poisoning. Did she know that?

The smell of camphor begins to burn in my nostrils, as I get closer to uncovering the maroon box. I jump and almost scream out loud when mothballs roll out of my father's old red McGill sweater. The M on the front is missing. I snipped it off and wore the sweater to high school when I was in grade nine. It was right in fashion, big and long enough to let just a fringe of Blackwatch tartan pleats show beneath it. I used to sneak out of the house in it so no one would know I'd been snooping in the Tuscaloosa trunk.

My father's old seersucker suit is wrapped in whispery tissue paper on top of the maroon box, the last piece of clothing.

Mother gave her wedding dress to Lily to be married in so it's not in here. I reach down to lift the suit out. My skin crawls. I swat at a tickle on my neck. My fingers tingle. I shove the suit aside, grit my teeth, shut my eyes, and lift the lid off the box.

Something is watching me. The spider.

A large black and white close-up photograph of a spider is lying on top of the cases of slides. Bulbous eyes stare back at me. Two black holes look like nostrils. Its mouth appears to be set in an angry grin; its poison claws are curved daggers above long venom sacs that hang down between two of its eight legs.

Lest you forget: Goldenberg is written in black ink on a length of blurred white the spider is sitting on. I sit on the cold grey cement floor and examine it in the beam of my flashlight for a long time. I squint. Then, heart pounding, I realize the writing is on the back of a left hand and the spider is on the little finger. I turn the photo over and see my father's neat printing: *Spider #111.33 – The Culprit! Photo by G.G. Goldenberg 10:47 a.m., Nov.12, 1933.*

Crying now, I put everything back the way I found it and close the lid of the trunk. Then I creep upstairs to bed.

It's the first Sunday morning after my father's death.

Campaigns

Anonym tells us the PAT answer to the old adage that love is blind is 20-20 EYEsight. We do not have a pat answer for which Pat in the pack of Pats at Central learned this love lesson in detention.

That item would have appeared in the gossip column of Central's newspaper *The Perroquet* if I'd had the nerve to send it after Eyeball's brown eyes met my blue eyes in detention. I knew I'd fallen in love when he winked at me and my heart fluttered like a cage full of doves. But we didn't fall into each other's arms there and then.

He already had a girlfriend, one who looked a lot like me. Her friends mistook me for her sometimes and teachers called me by her name. It was maddening. Double trouble was the last thing I needed. She definitely wasn't one of the glamour girls with so many guys on the string she wouldn't miss one. Neither was I. Eyeball took her to movies at the Capital Theatre Friday nights and they'd been seen together Sundays at Holy Rosary Cathedral – a sure sign they were getting serious about each other.

The only girl I told about my dream of going steady with a Greek god called Eyeball was Dene. She was the best friend I'd left behind in Lakeview School after I skipped a grade and started Central a year ahead of her. It was fair game for a high school girl to religiously stalk a Greek god, we decided. Dene agreed to sneak off with me one Sunday morning to see what went on at a Roman Catholic Mass. We sat at the back of the cathedral.

We'd heard that Catholic women wore head scarves to church instead of hats, never had time to take off their aprons, and had varicose veins that made their lisle stockings look as if they were filled with knotted ropes – a condition they suffered from because the Pope made them have so many babies. To us, they didn't look any different than Anglican, Presbyterian or United Church ladies, although some of them did have enough children tagging along with them to fill a pew.

A friend of Dene's older sister warned us not to let anyone know we weren't Roman Catholics. She said nice Protestant girls who got caught gawking at Dogans while they worshipped their idols were turned over to the nuns and melted down for altar candles. We laughed and said we weren't going to make spectacles of ourselves. Trying not to almost smothered us to death.

Our fits of contagious giggles started when a parade of priests and altar boys walked up the middle aisle and the leader shook water on everyone from what looked like a wizard's wand. We had to cover our mouths with both hands as we watched the head priest at the altar swinging a smoking silver container back and forth on a chain as if it was too hot to handle and he was going to sling it into the congregation. The ringing of what Dene whispered was the tinkliest fire bell she'd ever heard, and the priest daintily dipping his fingertips in a bowl of water and then touching them on a towel the altar boy held caused us to have sacrilegious seizures of muffled snickers. Every time we got our giggles under control, we would look at each other, or everyone else would suddenly sit down, or drop to their knees, and leave us standing up like a pair of plaster statues, and that would get us going again. I had to pinch my nose between my fingers to make sure I didn't snort. A couple of women in front of us turned and gave us dirty looks. A little girl spun around and stuck out her tongue. A boy old enough to know better picked something from his nose and snapped it at us with his fingers.

My heart flip-flopped and my giggling stopped when I saw Eyeball off to one side at the front. I poked Dene in the ribs and hissed at her to smarten up. He was sitting beside his brother Eye Junior in a row of men.

I thought that was a good sign, which it was.

My prayers to meet Eye Senior were answered on opening day of Central's 3-day election campaign for a new Student Council.

ELECTION DAZE
Wednesday, May 17, 1944
I arrived at campaign headquarters in Daph's garage before 5 a.m. to catch a ride to Central with an Atlas supporter.

Daph had recruited me to represent Track and Field in her chorus line that would dance ahead of Atlas's float in the election parade Friday through downtown Regina. Our yell was a cinch to memorize:

> *Live fast, faster, fastest*
> *Vote Atlas, Atlas, Atlas*

Revive our old athletic corpse
Vote Atlas Thomson in for sports
Our Central Titan's here at last
Vote Atlas! Atlas! Atlas!

The dance routine was hard to learn. Daph gave me a carbon copy of her choreography chart to study, but it looked like algebra. The cheer and demonic dance steps were to be repeated non-stop for the entire two miles of the parade route – but that wasn't until Friday.

On opening day the posters would go up in the main hall and the first campaigners inside the school would win the best spots. Some senior campaigners always made plans to spend the night at the school in sleeping bags to be at the front of the line. Vas, Frankie Sinatra's double and the Queen City's jitterbug king, let me squeeze into his older brother's Hudson on his second trip to Central. We got there about five forty-five. The sun was up, but two days of dust storms had stained the sky manure brown. Scarth Street was jammed for a block with kids and cars belching more kids out windows and doors and over the running boards and fenders. Campaigners were packed like sardines up the wide steps to the bank of teachers' doors, back down the sidewalk and across the street. Somewhere in the bowels of Central, two nervous janitors were waiting to open the doors at seven o'clock as a special concession to Election Daze fever.

Vas wasn't able to honk a spot clear of kids close to the curb near the mobbed entrance. Parts of posters were visible through the streamlined windows of the Hudson. We couldn't see all of the printed slogans, but we could hear enough of the cheers to figure them out. "IT'S TREASON NOT TO VOTE FOR REESON." "VOTE

FOR CELIA, SHE WON'T DOUBLE-DEAL YUH!" We shouted, "ATLAS FOR SPORTS!" over and over.

Norma and I climbed up on the Hudson's roof and saw Daph in the third row of the crush at the doors. She didn't seem to have the biggest and best Atlas poster.

I was just going to slide off the roof when Vas yelled, "Hey, look – it's a bird, it's a plane, it's Superman!" Vas was on the hood of the car, pointing his cigar toward the indelible sky over Central's entrance.

I tipped my head back and searched the sky. There had been rumours Atlas was going to make a parachute jump as part of his campaign. With a clank of bangles around her wrist, Colleen grasped my chin with her hand, turned my head toward the school, and said, "On the roof, above the teachers' door – see?"

I gasped. Atlas was shinnying up the flagpole and Eyeball was trying to hold it steady as it bent and swayed from side to side. Halfway up the pole, Atlas hung on with his legs, and wind-milling his arms, called to the hushed crowd, "Friends, Romans and Central-mites, the world's greatest election campaign is now open."

Cheers greeted his announcement. He slid down the flag-pole, and they both began to cavort along the roof's rim like per-formers in a high-wire circus act. Atlas did a cartwheel and a per-fect handstand while Eyeball held his ankles, and then they bowed at the crowd. I was thinking how much Eyeball looked like Clark Gable would without a moustache when he hunched his shoulders, blubbed out his lips, grunted loudly, scratched under his arms, and became an orangutan.

"Hey," Colleen said, "he did that last July First at B-Say-Tah Beach. Pulled a big dead tree across the road and stopped the traffic. The Fort Qu'Appelle newspaper said 'Mounties Seek Mysterious Apeman.'"

While Eyeball sprang around making monkey motions as if he was going to jump into the fir tree thirty feet away, Atlas did push-ups along the edge of the roof three storeys above the cement steps. I couldn't look. It was quiet enough to hear some ghoul say, "They're gonna fall – splat!" before the throng surged forward. The janitors had opened the doors early.

The first thing I saw inside was the huge Atlas poster hung in the choicest spot between the doors to the Library and the Detention Room. Daph stood beside it smiling.

She said, "The rooftop stunt was the signal they'd been in to hang it."

I signalled V for victory to her and threaded my way back outside. Satch, the Robinson Street dreamboat, was leaning against the front door of Vas's car, smoking a cigarette.

He called, "Hey, Butterball, coming for coffee? We're going to the Bus Depot."

I landed in the crowded back seat, sitting on Eyeball's lap. Not sitting, exactly, sort of crouching sideways with my feet tiptoe on the floor next to his so he wouldn't get the full impact of my weight.

Satch turned around and made the introduction. He said, "Butterball meet Eyeball. Don't break his knees."

"Hi," I said, and wondered if he could hear my heart doing cartwheels. "Eyeball's a funny name, how'd you get that?"

"This glass eye," he said, rolling his left eye up so only the white showed under the lid. "Want to see it?" He cupped his fingers around his eye as if he was going to remove an egg from a nest.

"No, no," I said, "I'd rather not, thanks."

"Why are you called Butterball?" he asked.

My knees melted. He got my whole weight without a gasp. Did I seem less "sturdy" to him than to my mother's bridge club – maybe even thin to someone with only one eye?

He didn't wait for an answer. "With your patrician profile, why isn't your nickname Cleo*pat*ra or Nefertiti? I've admired it in detention."

I touched the tip of my patrician profile and made a wish I would say something sensible.

I stared at Eyeball's eyes. They both looked warm and inviting – and real. My father said boys that tease me like me. All I could manage to say was, "Do you think it's a good idea to cram for final exams?"

"Sure. That's a time saver too. Only two weeks of studying to make up for kibitzing all year long."

I knew that would be his answer. I said, "That's exactly what I figured out." Then I asked, "Do you dance?"

He rolled the pupil of his left eye out of sight again, and said, "Not if I can avoid it. I went to the Freshie dance when I started Central and when they had a Paul Jones I hid behind the chairs at the back of the auditorium. Saved me from dancing one step all night."

We laughed.

He did another glass eye wink, and said, "Okay, I'll tell you the truth. I don't really have a glass eye. I discovered I could roll my eyes up like this..." (he demonstrated) "to look like glass. My kid brother's called Eyeball Junior, but he can only cross his eyes and he can't even wiggle his ears – like this – at the same time."

"I've got an eye trick too," I said. "It's not as complicated or clever as yours – it's really sort of corny." I leaned my head closer to his and showed him how I could press either eyeball into the inside corner next to my patrician profile and make it squeak. He laughed and got me to repeat the feat several times.

While the others had coffee, we sat side by side in the back seat of the car talking about life. We solved all the problems of the universe except where and when we were fated to meet again. It wouldn't be in detention because being late for assembly to hear speeches by the candidates wasn't as big a deal as skipping a class. Anyway, after having an intimately private heart-to-heart talk in the back seat of a car it would've been frustrating to sit at separate desks and just play silent eye-tricks – but better than nothing.

When the vote was held and the ballots were counted, Atlas won Sports – in either a close race or landslide, depending on which rumour you believed.

I missed the Victors and Vanquished Election Dance and 20-20 EYE sightings, but I had been promoted to grade ten without having to write any exams, and I'd enjoy two months of summer at the family cottage with my heart pitter-pattering during practise romances with cute boys my own age while I secretly planned my 1944-45 Eyeball campaign.

The big date took until February 1945 to win. Eyeball was slipping out the side door of Central as I was going back in. I'd just decided not to skip Latin anymore in case he invited me to go to Mass with him sometime. He leaned against the doorjamb and asked me to the Queen City Skating Club Sweethearts Ball on Saturday night.

It was a formal, and Dene's older sister loaned me her long dress with the black velveteen skirt and the red plaid taffeta bodice. The pink sweetheart rose corsage Eyeball brought me clashed, but I wore it anyway. I still have it pressed in wax paper between the pages of my high school diary.

We won the last spot dance, a sign if we stuck together we would be lucky in love, I thought. The prize was from Birks Jewellers: a bone china teacup and saucer in a petit point rose pattern. I tucked it away in the hope chest Grandma Blair had given me when I graduated from grade eight; it was the first thing I'd put in it that had sentimental value.

The weekend after the Sweetheart Ball, Dene's sister saw Eyeball holding hands with his old girlfriend in the long Friday night line up outside the Capital Theatre for the movie *Since You Went Away*. She had the nerve to be mad at *me* about it. She said it had really mortified her when she tapped his girlfriend on the back and said, "Well, if it isn't Pat Blair with the Eye she stole from her double," and then realized it wasn't me.

I carried the royal blue Birks box down the basement to our furnace room, took the teacup and saucer out of their tissue bed, and smashed them against the cement wall in the coal bin. I felt my heart cracking into petit point chips as I did it, but I vowed that was that for dating a cheating Catholic.

Eyeball phoned me the next Friday after school. We went to the Broadway Theatre and saw the rerun of *For Whom The Bell Tolls* that night. Saturday afternoon we walked the four blocks from my house to Regina Avenue to catch the bus to the Airport Inn to have milkshakes, watch the airplanes and talk, and he accepted Mother's invitation to come for our ritual roast beef dinner Sunday night.

We were going steady.

But how did I know it was true love?

I ate perogies at his house without throwing up.

Of course I knew Stan – Eyeball Junior – to say hello to at Central, but it was the first time I'd met Frank's parents, his older sister Agnes, her husband Peter Schick, and their sons Barry, Bob and Tom. Frank was always boasting about what great perogies his mom made for Friday night suppers. I didn't have a clue what he was talking about. I thought they might be special Catholic dumplings in a meatless vegetable stew.

Everyone sat down at the dining room table except Frank's mother. There was a place set for her, but Mrs. Krause didn't sit down and eat with us; she just served us.

At my house, after my father died, my mother sat at his end of the table to carve the meat, and I took over at Mother's end and served the vegetables from the silver entree dishes. Passing plates from one end of the table to the other to have them filled had to be done correctly. It kept us all busy until everyone was served, the blessing was said, and my mother lifted her cutlery to indicate we could take our first bite.

At Frank's house it was different. Empty plates were already set at our places when we went to the table. A blessing was said while we stood behind our chairs, the family slashed the sign of the cross on their chests, sat down, and everyone began eating as soon as Mrs. Krause put food on their plates – except me.

Mrs. Krause leaned over my shoulder and served me first. I couldn't believe that what slid off the ladle onto my plate was cooked. It looked like half-moon pouches of raw dough.

Frank's father was seated next to me, on the side of the table farthest away from the steamy kitchen. He spooned blobs of sour cream on top of the raw dough on my plate before I could ask him to stop.

Sour cream? My mother would have cooked it in Tuscaloosa biscuits or bran muffins – or flushed it down the toilet.

Agnes reached around her father and laid a pile of limp fried onion strings over the whole mess on my plate. I watched them settle into the gooey white topping. It was white everything; tablecloth, plates, food, my face. Milky white curds of cottage cheese spilled out of the perogies when I finally had to burrow into them with my fork. Most of the family were ready for their second helpings by then. My eyes watered every time I tried to swallow a bite.

"Like them?" Frank kept asking me.

I nodded my head, ever so slightly, afraid I might spit up what I was trying to chew – and the stuff partway down my throat too.

"Mom's the best perogy maker in the universe," Stan said as she filled his plate again.

"Grandma says you ate twenty-eight of them once and you have the record so far, Uncle Stan," Barry said.

"Lots more in the kitchen. Don't be afraid to dig in," Mr. Krause said. He smiled at me. A horrible curd was caught at his gum line over his eye tooth.

"Mom's recipe makes a thousand," Frank said.

The napkins were just paper serviettes, too thin to hide anything. I hadn't spoken a word during the whole meal. When I finally swallowed the last bite, Mrs. Krause asked if I'd like more. To my shock, holding the crumpled serviette close to my mouth,

I heard myself say, "Yes, please. Just a few more if you're sure you've got enough."

As Mr. Krause reached for the bowls, I quickly said, "Without sour cream and onions, thank you. These are the most delicious perogies I've ever eaten. They don't need any garnishes."

Mrs. Krause taught me how to make perogies the summer we decided to get married. It took us all one Friday morning to make the dough, roll it out, cut, fill, and pinch together the edges. And we spent all afternoon standing over pots of boiling water waiting for the egg-size pouches to bob to the surface while we prayed none of them would come apart. My aching legs told me that perogy-making probably caused more varicose veins than the Pope's rule against any form of birth control that worked.

I quartered half her recipe and quadrupled the size when I made perogies by myself. "Anglo-Saxon perogies," Frank called them, and said one of mine was as delicious as six of his mother's.

My mother wasn't upset when I told her I wanted to marry Frank. She'd grown fond of him. It didn't bother her that it would be a mixed marriage. I overheard my father's older brother tell her it was a disgrace to allow me to drag a Pope-lover into the Blair clan. Mother told him to hang onto his fedora because she was seeing a Roman Catholic widower who had twelve children. She said much the same thing to her oldest brother, who'd been given the family farm, house, stock and mineral rights, except she changed the hat to a John Deere cap and the widower to a bachelor farmer with four sections of wheat fields studded with pumping oil wells.

Frank and I decided to elope for a lot of reasons. Mother had sold the house and she was busy getting ready to move to an apartment with Heather when one became available in Devon Court, a former three-storey family home converted to six suites, not far from Lakeview School. Frank and I thought a wedding reception would make us feel as if we were the fake bride and groom on the top tier of a fancy cake. We worried about how comfortable it would be for the Krause family to make small talk with my Blair and Wilson relatives and vice versa. Without my gregarious father to break the ice, Mother and Frank and I agreed the formality would be no fun for anyone.

The five hundred dollars Mother offered us to elope was all we needed to tear up the tentative guest list. We decided to take the money and run. There was only one hitch. I had to finish my lessons in the Roman Catholic faith first.

Father O'Hara looked like an Orangeman's version of a Roman Catholic priest: too obese from rich food to be anything other than celibate, except maybe with the nuns; dressed in a long black skirt and wearing jewellery; blinking the bloodshot eyes of an altar wine guzzler.

Maybe he did nip at the wine. He had a flushed face with scribbles of broken blood vessels on his nose and cheeks. And there was a faint odour of sulphur about him that made me hold my breath.

Frank had to come with me to my three lessons to renew his faith because he intended to marry outside the church. Father

O'Hara treated him like a juvenile delinquent and called me either "chee-ild" or a "Protestant" as if he'd mispronounced the world's oldest profession.

It made me argumentative. Was he accusing me of seducing a nice Catholic boy? Luring him away from a good Catholic girl into a life of sin? Maybe he knew Frank's old girlfriend from hearing her confessions. I hoped so. I hoped she bored him as much as she'd bored Frank.

"I've been fitted with a diaphragm," I told Father O'Hara as I signed the pledge to bring up *Frank's* children in the Roman Catholic faith. "Frank wants to buy an Austin car before we have a baby."

Father O'Hara belched, glared at Frank, and crossed himself.

"I feel it's my responsibility not to get pregnant on my wedding night while I'm doing my duty as a wife," I said. "Protestant girls are brought up not to leave everything to God." I gave him my most saintly smile.

"My poor chee-ild..." Father O'Hara clasped his hands together and made a steeple with his index fingers. "Frank would be committing adultery to lie with a girl who uses the temple of her body for lust and fornication instead of holy procreation."

"Oh, but we'll be joined in holy matrimony," I said.

"The use of birth control places a Catholic soul in mortal sin."

"But confession would –"

"Absolution would not be given. Never! The sacraments would be denied to such a Catholic sinner."

I looked at Frank. He crossed himself and winked at me. *I* did not have a Roman Catholic soul to be stained with indelible sin in the line of duty.

The sun shone on our elopement day. My mother took a snapshot of us before we left for the rectory and we're both squinting in it.

H ow do we know we're in love? This is my *Frank Pat* answer – pun intended.

True love is shouting matches and angry silences and making up tenderly. It is laughing at each other's corny jokes, witty repartee exchanged after the party's over, and widening the path through a jungle of contradictions so there's room for two adventurers. True love is a tangerine tent that can't be torn down by a gale or tornado, blizzard or hurricane, pitched on top of a steep hill.

And true love is dancing toward dawn on New Year's Eve, after the party is over, necking with my old high school sweetheart and dancing, oh, so slowly, to Glenn Miller's "Sentimental Journey." Once, as we glided across the kitchen, Frank dipped me back and there she was, our eight-year-old daughter Barbara Jane, her pretty wide-eyed face in front of mine, upside down. She'd heard the soft music after all the guests left and sneaked downstairs to her special spying place under the breakfast nook table with the dog.

We coaxed her out, held her between us, and danced until the record ended.

Bed Making

It's 9 a.m., Monday, August 7, 1950, and the sun is radiant. I'm ready, eager, and a bit scared. The crunch of tires on gravel will announce Frank's arrival to pick me up. I stand in the doorway to memorize my maidenhood bedroom.

My bed and pillows look so forlorn stripped to the ticking. Changing my bed on an ordinary Monday morning meant I put the bottom sheet down the laundry chute and replaced it with the top sheet I'd slept under for a week. The new sheet and pillow slips from the linen closet had always been ironed as smooth as silk by my mother and smelled of *Rinso* soap flakes. Going back to bed instead of off to school or work was a temptation. Not today. Knowing I'll never again sleep here in this room makes me feel as if I got up before I went to bed.

Mother helped me fold my blankets and bedspread and whisked them away to one of her moving boxes. She's going to store my bedroom furniture at her mother's, in Grandma Sophie's attic in Indian Head, until Frank and I are living somewhere that has a bedroom, not just a Murphy bed. Changing my bed this morning means to one with Frank in it. If leaving an unmade bed is bad luck, I hope being dressed for good luck cancels it.

I'm wearing something old – and easy to take off. My stockings are new and seamless, like Frank and I will be after we're married an hour from now. Mother's white cotton gloves are borrowed. Something blue is not the usual ruffled lace garter a bride at a big wedding ceremony takes off and tosses to her husband's bachelor friends. A baby blue case is hidden in the bottom of my purse. It contains my wand, a tube of sealing jelly that also lubricates, and protected in its own round blue compact, my custom fitted *Ortho* diaphragm.

I got my diaphragm after passing the doctor's test on correct preparation, insertion, removal and post-coital care. I practised on my last five celibate nights. The gynaecological position required is an awkward partial sit-up, knees bent and spread, pelvis raised, loaded wand in one hand, the other hand flat on the bed for support. I barricaded the closed door of this entry to my inner sanctum, splayed out on my chenille bedspread half-naked with my nightgown rolled up at my waist, and slid it in. I'm getting slicker and quicker at plugging my "well of life" (the pseudonym for uterus it's rumoured nuns teach Catholic girls), but I feel a bit jittery about tonight – or maybe this afternoon.

There's a question I intended to ask Frank. Are Roman Catholic boys brought up to believe we'll become one flesh tonight by me being cleaved unto? Sexual intercourse sounds more mutual and, said slowly in a whispery voice, more romantic. I expect consummating our marriage to be a shared reward for all the times we stopped short of going all the way. I think we'll both want to do it every chance we get. Finding a private place in a bachelor suite to put in my diaphragm will be a challenge. In the bathtub perhaps? But that won't be mine alone either.

Where does a married woman go to be alone? Stomping off to the refuge of my bedroom and slamming the door on the world was the cold compress on my hot forehead that allowed me to think things through. Retreating here quietly and closing the door softly allowed me to cry, gloat, preen, dream, and ask myself tough questions. Giving up my private domain is a leap of faith in more ways than one.

A stranger standing here now wouldn't see any evidence this room once sheltered a nine-year-old girl homesick for Toronto. There aren't any signs of her metamorphosis to a Queen City teen swimming upstream in pursuit of a dreamboat called Eyeball – whose name Frank Ernest fits his personality – to today's bride, age twenty, who can't stop wondering how it's going to feel as she becomes an ex-virgin and imagining things she'll do to make it exciting for her husband to lose his virginity to her at the same time, like if she....

I should go downstairs right now; turn slowly in the kitchen doorway so Mother can admire the alterations to my skirt. Wonder how to cook a meal. Imagine a menu. Read Mother's recipe books. Start a grocery list. Lack of sleep has made me antsy about tonight.

Last night, I thrashed around until dawn in this bed of mine that I've stripped as stark naked as it was when the store delivered it. I was trying to kick out a horde of invaders, shouting, "Cleave unto her! Split! Rend apart! Rive! Penetrate!" My mother and father appeared at my bedside wearing their wedding clothes and everything was okay. I wasn't cut in two. I was alone in bed. I'd almost fallen back asleep when my parents began to bounce on my bed and singsong over and over: Oh, it's so much fun/making two halves one.... After breakfast this morning, Mother cut cucumber slices for me to put on my crinkled eyelids, but my bedclothes weren't even rumpled.

When I was nine and pining for my friends in Toronto, my father taught me how to make my new bed in Regina as tight as a tourniquet.

"Nobody ever fell out of a bed or a sleeping car berth I made," he boasted. "Watch my bedside manner."

"I wish you'd bought me a flying carpet so I could fly home to Toronto to go to bed," I said.

"I looked at a few oriental rugs, but your mother claims they're always wrinkled. What if you stood up to navigate over Lake Ontario, tripped and fell off?"

"I'd swim to shore and walk home to Saint Leonard's Avenue," I said. "And I'd go back to Blythewood School in the morning."

"Well, stay home with us, and you'll be snug as a bug in a rug in this spooled walnut dream ship. It won't spill you out once I teach you my Pullman porter's tricks of bed making."

"It's too damn wide for me to make. See? I can't even reach across it." I leaned over and stretched out my arm.

"Dam the damns, young lady. Don't get cold feet without trying. Beds fit for a princess have to be as big as a kingdom. You can learn to mitre corners so your sheets and blankets stay tucked. Your feet will be warm as toast all night long."

He mitred a corner while I watched, pulled it apart, and I practised doing it twice. After I did all eight corners of the sheets and two blankets, my father gave me an A-plus, and said my next challenge was putting on pillow slips correctly.

"When placing pillows in slips, do not hold the slip or the pillow with your teeth or chin. Clamping with your teeth makes you look like a cartoon beaver." He demonstrated the look.

I laughed.

"Chin-clamps scrunch up your face, and a frog prince seeking your kiss would garumph and leap away." He garumphed like a tuba and leapt away from me. "Worse," he said, stepping back beside me, "both methods are damn unsanitary."

"Why?" I asked.

"The pillow slipper can spread germs to the pillow sleeper from her mouth or nose." He cupped his hands in front of his face and sneezed uproariously.

"And from his hands if he doesn't wash them," I said.

We both soaped and scrubbed our hands and arms to our elbows as he'd taught us to do before what he called "surgical sleight of hand" jobs such as making a peanut butter and banana sandwich. When we returned to my bedroom, he told me to stand beside him, listen to his instructions, and follow his actions.

"Lay the pillow on the bed in front of you. Grip the slip at the open end. Reach across the length of the pillow. Hold it behind the tail feathers. And capture it in the sack!"

I got the pillow in the slip on my first try.

"Okay. Great catch. Now, reach inside and poke the pillow into the corners."

I finished first, and we played the Favourite Game he plays with my mother and brother, too.

He said, "I'm proud to declare you won the 1939 Pillow Slip Competition. Without a doubt, you are my favourite daughter."

"I'm your only daughter," I said, which I still was then.

He feigned delighted surprise. "Really? Wise me. My one and *only* favourite daughter and I will now compete in the fun part of making a bed. We shall fluff our pillows by striking them vigorously with our open hands before placing them on this majestic bed."

We smacked our pillows harder and harder, laughed and garumphed, then picked them up and had a pillow fight. Mother came in to see what the ruckus was about. We put our pillows on my bed, my parents praised my bed-making skills, and Mother showed me how to tuck the bedspread under the pillows to centre the three blue chenille morning glory blossoms.

After that, making my bed every morning was something I was expected to do. It became a parental myth that I could mitre a corner and fluff a feather pillow better than a Pullman porter.

My father told two railroad stories I loved to hear. The true one about him being a porter had a happy ending.

He had a little rhyme to begin the story: "My ache wasn't caused by something I ate / and a westbound train in nineteen twenty-eight / was just what the doctor ordered." The time was right. He'd just finished interning in Montreal, had landed his first medical position there as a pathology instructor at McGill University in the fall, when he sought the summer job as a porter. His turnaround at Regina, his hometown, gave him a three-day layover to touch base with his family and court my mother in person again.

At the end of June, he arranged for his turnaround to be at my mother's hometown of Indian Head so they could get married. After a short honeymoon at the Fort Qu'Appelle Hotel, they took separate trains to Montreal. "Hardest three nights I spent as a porter with no relief," my father used to say, and wink at my blushing mother. The wink and blush were a mystery to me until I'd read *Forever Amber* at fourteen and then found an explanation of the erectile and flaccid penis in my father's *Gray's Anatomy*. Facts slapped a cold blanket on the tempestuous romances of Amber St. Clare, but not on the true romance of my parents.

The sad railroad story my father told was a crying song he called "a reverse fairy tale" that he began by playing his sleight-of-hand harmonica. He held his hands around his mouth, exhaled and inhaled into them, and produced the sounds of a train chugging along the track, its whistle, and the tune. Then he sang the lyrics of the "Wreck Of The Number Nine," did a mournful train whistle that was a wordless prayer, and sang the last verse. As the brave engineer lies dying in the wreckage, he sends this message to the maiden he was going to wed: "There's a little white home / I bought for our own / Where I dreamed we'd be happy bye and bye / And I leave it to you / for I know you'll be true / Till we meet at that golden gate, goodbye."

I've known all the words off by heart since I was two years old, but I never sang the last verse with my father.

As a child, I asked why God let the brave engineer die. My father told me God didn't, a talented Kansas hillbilly singer-songwriter named Carson Robison made up the story and tune.

As a girl, I had much more to be sad about than a song. Canada declared war on Germany on Sunday, September 10, 1939. Three years later, on Monday, September 14, 1942, Grandma Blair received the dreaded telegram about the youngest of her four sons, Jack. On the flight back to England after bombing German factories, his Lancaster was shot down over Cologne. Uncle Jack had taught me to play tennis and had opened a savings account for me at Huron and Erie Trust where he worked until he joined the RCAF. "Smiling Jack," my father called him. At the family gathering, he read what was in Central's 1927 yearbook about Jack when he was sixteen in grade eleven: *Jack Blair is why girls leave home.* That was the only time I ever saw my father cry. Uncle Jack wasn't married and I wondered if a true-hearted girl was waiting for brave Smiling Jack to come home from the war to wed her.

Just thinking about it makes my throat hurt holding back tears. It used to be that when I heard a train on the Lewvan Line while I was cloistered up here in my room, I thought of the song and had what my mother calls "a good cry." Since my father's death almost two years ago, just imagining the sound of a train whistle makes me shut my windows.

Today, as a woman about to be married to my true love, I've opened my bedroom windows so wide I can hear my father in heaven whistling, "Oh What A Beautiful Morning."

The landscape outside the west window of my second-storey bedroom is as flat as a map. The return address in my diary ends: *Canada, North America, World, Universe.* The close-up details are a mixture of fact and fiction. Until after the war, ours was the last house on the southwest corner of Regina, and a block away from the nearest houses to the north and east. Although the *Arabian Nights* architecture makes our house resemble a *Hill* Avenue outpost of *Lakeview,* there isn't any hill and it's too far from Wascana Lake to see Regina's man-made oasis. Growing up out here, I had to call on my friends to go anywhere and be on time so they didn't go without me. Still, I feel really lucky to have lived in the midst of all the heavenly bodies in the universe.

The view from my west window is over an ocean of ever-changing prairie to a farmhouse and the airport. During the war, my imaginary love was a handsome RCAF pilot who flew by my isolated tower window at sunset and dipped the wings of his golden Tiger Moth to blow me kisses. Now, the handsome guy I'm marrying today works at the airport checking in Trans-Canada Airline passengers. As he drives over here to carry me away in his father's car, he'll be thinking of flying high with me in his arms. Tonight, while wondrous dreams come true in our honeymoon bed, the beacon on the airport tower will sweep its bright circular path across this empty room.

Looking out my north window, I see the twin spires of Holy Rosary Cathedral. We're taking our vows in the dark inquisition room of the rectory where Father O'Hara asked Frank about my religious background. I told him that in 1944, when I was fourteen and my Presbyterian father was forty-four, we'd taken catechism lessons together and been confirmed in my mother's Anglican church. He closed his eyes, frowned, and stated that legally two become one in a mixed marriage, but not spiritually in the eyes of the Holy See. Frank did his glass eye trick.

I look around the chaste maiden's sanctum I'm vacating today for true love – and lust.

I see a closet with a door, not a curtain. Me crowding in among the clothes and pushing aside saddle shoes, loafers, moccasins, runners and sandals to lie down on the floor during a slumber party challenge. Pretending when I come out I was bold and brave and modern enough to insert a tampon. Saying it feels great; I'll never use a scratchy pad again. Nobody knows I'm the only one who still hasn't gotten the curse.

My dressing table. Its swinging side mirrors let me study my profile from both sides and long to have my so-called patrician nose bobbed and the bump smoothed out.

The bookcases flanking my desk are barren. My father's set of Edgar Allan Poe and two big thick copies of *The Girl's Own Annual* that Mother's double-cousin in England sent to her when they were girls are already in the small bookcase in our apartment.

My chest of drawers is empty. While I was at work last week, Mother and her friend, Mrs. Art, moved its contents to our apartment and arranged it all on my half of the shelves in the long narrow walk-in closet where the bed goes when it's swung up. The only thing I couldn't find was the package of my waist-length braids that were cut off when I was twelve so I could start grade eight with a sophisticated Katharine Hepburn pageboy. Nobody else was at home to witness the scene about my missing hair. My sister Heather, who's ten, is in Edmonton with our aunt and cousins until the end of August. When she comes back, her home and Mother's will be with Grandma Sophie in Indian Head. My brother Kenny, eighteen months younger than I am, has a job at Imperial Oil and moved into a boarding house last month. I do the office work at Mac & Mac Menswear, a few minutes walk from our bachelor suite, which Frank and I visited before he dropped me off at home to change my clothes for our last Saturday night date before we're wed.

Mother was in the living room sitting in her rocking chair doing nothing. I kicked off my shoes, sat down in my father's chair, and put my bare feet up on his footstool.

"Frank and I sure think you and Mrs. Art did a super job organizing everything," I said. "Where did you put the package of my hair?"

"In the garbage," Mother said. She stopped rocking.

"Oh, sure." I smiled.

"So it wouldn't breed–"

"With the horsehair in that ancient mattress I inherited from Great-aunt Janet on the Murphy bed?" I laughed.

"Moths." She began rocking furiously.

"Ha-ha. Nothing could breed in the stinky mothballs you piled on them, but dumping them in the garbage is not funny."

"Well, we did. We thought–"

"We? We? You and who? God? Mrs. Art?" I took my feet off the footstool. "And you think two heads are better than one? You're the one who knows damn well why I kept them. My father took me to the Hotel Saskatchewan beauty salon to have my hair cut and styled in a pageboy. He said just because his favourite eldest daughter was brilliant enough to skip grade seven didn't mean she had to look like a child genius. You stood there like the Dutch Cleanser lady and said pigtails were neat and tidy and kept the hair out of the eyes of agile Hollywood stars like Sonja Henie and Esther Williams."

Mother's hands were hovering over her ears. "Attached to your head, yes. Wrapped in tissue paper in a dark hope chest from a good housekeeping perspective–"

"Then he took me to lunch in the hotel dining room, just the two of us, to celebrate. And you and Mrs. Art-fart decided my braids didn't matter to me anymore because my father's dead? He gave me the red plaid ribbons tied on them. I was going to stuff a pillow with that hair someday."

My eyes got watery. So did Mother's. We faced each other silently.

Then Mother put her hands over her eyes, and said, "Both of us moving is, well, hard on the nerves. I made a mistake. I'm sorry. Your hair was yours to keep. I shouldn't have decided to throw your braids away. My decision was wrong." She clasped her hands together on her lap. "I don't know. If the furnace didn't need to be changed to oil and...."

"We don't need the five hundred dollars you gave us to elope," I said. "Frank saved two hundred dollars when he worked at International Harvester. We'll be okay without it."

Mother shook her head. "No, no, the money's yours. A big wedding would have cost twice as much. I want you to keep it. Your father would, too. It's the right time for me to sell the house – my bank manager will buy it for eighteen thousand dollars. That's six thousand more than we paid for it. I've made up my mind to sell and that's that."

I thought of the bank manager as Mr. B.M. and expected him to look like Salvador Dali. I imagined him twisting the spiky ends of his moustache as he took advantage of poor widows. But yesterday he dropped by with his wife after church to show her what he'd bought, and he looks like Orson Welles playing black marketer Harry Lime in *The Third Man*. He calls his wife Pussy. It must be because of her hiss. When I asked her how many kids they had, she said, "We do not have any young goats," sucked air in through her teeth, and added, "Nor any children, either." She looked so superior after her little joke, I thought she was going to lie down on the upstairs hall rug and lick herself.

In my parent's bedroom, Pussy looked in the twin closets, smiled at herself in Mother's full-length mirror, and purred it would be her room. Then she crossed the hall, glanced into my room, and said it would be his. Mother covered her mouth and did her dry little cough to hide a snicker. I didn't try to disguise my snort, and thought: I cannot, will not, must not ever let myself imagine Mrs. Pussy in my parent's bedroom or Mr. B.M. in mine.

After they left, Mother said, "A fat cat makes her bed alone to prevent littering." I meowed, and we got the giggles.

I hear the crunch of gravel at exactly 9:30, blow a kiss into my room, turn, and run downstairs.

Frank and I stand side by side holding hands on the front lawn beside the fir tree while Mother takes snapshots of us.

"Isn't the mother of the bride supposed to cry on her daughter's wedding day?" I ask my smiling mother when Frank opens the car door for me.

Mother hugs me, and whispers, "You've made your bed well. Try to get a little sleep in it."

The priest who married us was a pleasant surprise. Father Mooney was slim and tall, dressed in a suit, and a lot younger and friendlier than Father O'Hara. He was surprised we hadn't been told to bring witnesses and recruited two altar ladies from the cathedral.

Then sunshine! Man and wife! Married! A permanent state till death do us part. I was Mrs. Frank Krause for the rest of my life and would never again be just plain Pat Blair.

"Do you think we did the right thing?" I asked in the car.

"Want to go back and ask Father for an annulment or head for the lake and get to bed early?" Frank did an eyeball roll.

At 11:30, we stopped in Indian Head to tell Gran Sophie and took her for a noon wedding dinner at the Rainbow Café. Uncle Jack and Aunt Marie Wilson and the hired couple on the farm, Pat and Irene Gibson, were in a booth. Grandma tapped her cane on the floor, and said, "May I introduce newly wed Mr. and Mrs. Frank Krause."

On Highway 57, eating dust for dessert on the last lap to the lake, I said, "Shit," and clamped my hand over my mouth. What kind of married lady uses words like that? "I mean, shoot. Oh, shoot, I forgot the cottage keys."

"Shall we turn back or break in?" Frank asked.

"Break in," we said in unison. And that's what we did. Frank shoved me through the small window over the coal oil stove and I unlatched the front door for him.

Bedtime was late evening. No bathtub, no indoor bathroom, no bedroom of my own. A sleeping porch fifty feet from the main cottage, a wash basin, covers to tent with my knees, a virgin husband waiting for the okay to turn around and face me.

Did Mother know that the slightest motion in the honeymoon bed would cause the brass spools on the head and foot rails to ring like wedding bells? The white wrought iron double bed was a relic from the boys' dormitory in Gran Sophie's attic, which Mother's three brothers had shared with farm schoolboys who couldn't get home in the winter. It had been a trampoline for acrobatics, home plate in cot-hopping games, a schooner that was sailed across walloping waves by a rollicking crew, and even a bed slept on by whoever stayed awake long enough to fight off pirates. The broken springs and sag in the mattress as deep as a coulee forced the bride and groom to cleave unto each other to consummate their marriage and, eventually, to achieve sexual intercourse.

All of a sudden it's Thursday, August 7, 1975, the 25th anniversary of Frank and me making our bed together both metaphorically and literally. For us, true love that's forever and fun is the result of rituals we've invented that stimulate the mundane tasks of homemaking, like the Pillow Slip War.

Once a week, Frank and I stand at our sides of the bed, our pillows on it in front of us, clean folded pillow slips lying on top of them. We are tense, on the mark, ready, set – Go! The one who gets the pillow in the slip first is the winner, the Night of Clean Sheets Aggressor. I am dextrous at putting a pillow slip on swiftly.

We're at the cottage today, as we are every year on this date, to toast promises kept – except for our pledge to have six children, not four. Each of our three daughters was here on August 7 in my womb and our son at a month old: Judy in '51, Jim '53, Barb '55, and Kathy 1960 – the year of our 10th anniversary. The cottage is full of family artefacts such as yearbooks and photograph albums.

Snapshots of my parents at their wedding reception in Grandma and Grandpa Wilson's yard fill one old album. In tiny black triangular corners on the black pages, there are front, back and sideways views of Mother modelling her swishy 1920s flapper wedding dress and floppy-brimmed hat and of her sitting in a weather-beaten wicker chair with the elderly curly-haired Wilson family mutt, Jeff, sitting at her knee gazing up at her. Jeff had ESP, Mother said. He was always waiting at the Indian Head train station when Mother arrived for unexpected weekend visits home from her teaching job at Gull Lake. In my favourite snapshot, the happy couple stand side by side in that old pals pose so popular in the Twenties. They each have one arm stretched out with that hand on the other one's shoulder; the bride's right hand is on her hip, the groom's left hand is thrust deep in his suit jacket pocket, and their legs are crossed in opposite directions as if they're propping each other up after dancing the Charleston. Underneath it, in the white ink he used on his spider slides, my father printed: *The Penniless Doc & His Bride – June 28, 1928.*

In *The Keystone,* the University of Saskatchewan yearbook back then, Mother's 1923 graduation photo in cap and gown is beside what it says about her:

FLORENCE MARY WILSON – ARTS
When she will, she will,
When she won't, she won't,
So there's an end on't.
Lots of pep, lots of go – that's Willy. She knows her
own mind and when she starts she goes right through.
As centre on the basketball team we have yet to find
another with her speed and skill.
Pet Saying: I don't care, I just won't do it.
Pastime: Hiking, not alone.
Present Ambition: To train for a nurse in Montreal.

. Like mother like daughter, I think about her ambition.

My father's graduation photo is in the 1924 yearbook. I suspect he wrote what it says about him and the activities of the medical students:

ALLAN WALKER BLAIR

Genus, – Medicanus doctorus. First found in Brussels, Ont. Then discovered in Regina in larva stage, feeding voraciously on secondary education, sport, and similar foods. Next found in pupa stage in university in colony Societas Medicana, carrying on important functions. Is also active outside the colony, his prey being organisms known as socii, rugbiani and basketballi. The adult stage should be found in Eastern Canada in the future.

True to their traditions, the Medical Society of the term 1923-24 again made their presence felt.

Shh! Ouch! Awful fate!
Dope him! Drug him! Operate!
Broken bones and busted heads –
Who are we? S'katchewan Meds.
Why did they kick that medical student out of the Library?
They caught him trying to remove the appendix from a book.

For twenty-five years I've wanted to know if Mother shed a few tears after we eloped, and at a family gathering I finally ask, "As mother of the bride not invited to the wedding ceremony, did you cry?"

She taps her wedding ring against her glass of champagne to get everyone's attention, takes some handwritten pages out of her purse, and says, "This is the marriage announcement I wrote and never sent to the *Leader-Post*." Then she reads:

"The bride's wedding day began at the Blair family home that used to be out on the bald prairie, but feels like the heart of the city now with the airport bus stop at the door, and wooden side-walks so planks don't have to be laid across the ditch to the gravel road.

"As usual, the bride had breakfast before applying her lipstick or taking the curling rags out of her hair. Later, she donned the pink linen two-piece dress she wore at her cousin's wedding two years ago. Her mother's dressmaker, Mrs. Zimmer, took the full-ness out of the skirt, which made it much more becoming. The bride wore a white pique cloche and the brown and white spec-tator pumps on her feet she'd worn to work all summer. For this occasion, she put on seamless stockings that matched her tan. Her white gloves were spotless because her mother washed them Sunday morning. Instead of a bouquet, she carried a large tan purse full of junk.

"The groom was attired in his navy blue blazer and grey trousers after a good deal of discussion as to whether this outfit or his grey flannel suit would be more appropriate. It was agreed that informality was the keynote of this wedding.

"The mother-of-the-bride wore her old blue Red Cross smock with the sleeves rolled up and her yellowed canvas runners she'd worn when she won the Gull Lake Singles Tennis Cup in 1924.

"The house was decorated with cartons of shoes, magazines, pots and pans, ornaments, and stacks of books in the vestibule and front hall. Two barrels packed with the good china were the centrepiece on the dining room table.

"After the bride's mother took a wedding day snapshot, the happy couple left for the ceremony and a three-day honeymoon at the Lake Katepwa family cottage without taking the keys.

"The groom drove his father's streamlined, two-tone grey, '47 Deluxe Torpedo Chev, packed with things for the cottage: a fireplace screen, coal scuttle, the bride's large childhood blackboard, cartons of Reader's Digests, National Geographics, old pocketbooks to reread, two bent lampshades, patched towels and sheets and pillow slips, and other valuable items.

"Upon their return, the happy couple will make their home in the Grenfell Apartments in the heart of downtown Regina.

"After the bride and groom's departure, the bride's mother retired to the basement to stoke the jacket heater and do the Monday washing.

"The end," Mother said. Everyone applauded.

"But there's more," Mother said. "When the laundry was hung, I went upstairs to pack the pictures in the bedroom I'd slept in with the father of the bride. I decided to take his University of Saskatchewan graduation photo out of the frame in case the movers broke the glass and damaged it. I took off the backing to remove his picture and found this hand-printed letter – a very special letter he'd put there when he framed it."

She unfolds two small pieces of paper. "Before I read it to you," she says, "I graduated in 1923 and had taught for a year when Allan graduated. He had pneumonia at exam time in '23 and didn't get his pre-med B.Sc. until 1924."

Mother reads the letter in her once-upon-a-time voice:

"Today is the 12th day of May 1924, a cold Monday, and this grad photo of me arrived this morning. I wonder if when this note is found it will only serve to recall dim distant dreams. I will always think of you as I do this morning – that you're the best friend I ever met, bar none.

"Years hence I shall recall hiding this note and we shall open it and read it together I hope. It was this spring that I first came to be absolutely sure that there was only one girl in the world for me.

"Last night I was at Curly's for supper and we had a talk on various things. In the course of our conversation he made a remark that pleased me tremendously. It was something like this: he had always figured that you and I were cut out for each other and that we would make a good pair. I hope with all that's in me that this is true and that its truth will be proven when we read this some day in the future.

"I am now a university graduate but still have three years till I am a medical doctor – the first goal of my dreams. This chap in the picture looks not so bad. It remains for me to accomplish something worthwhile.

"I put my photo beside your graduation photo and looked at the two as if I were a stranger to both. They look not so badly together. May it always be so.

"This is sure a fine world to live in. I am now going out to look for work – not a position. On the 24th I will see you again. Allan of 1924."

When she finishes, everyone is teary-eyed and smiling. Mother looks at me, and says, "After I'm dead you can use this in one of your stories."

I don't trust my voice and only nod my head.

The Lookout Stone

Going out of the valley, coming in, nothing is supposed to be hidden from view up here.

This rock is a special watching place on the hills around our old family cottage. It doesn't change. The yellow patches of lichen that roughen its bone-white surface, and the hollow footholds, one a step ahead of the other, still make it possible to sit here without sliding off down the steep slope.

I'm glad to sit down, catch my breath. How can the valley look so shallow, so much closer, and the climb to the Lookout Stone on Camel Back Hill seem so difficult now? Age? Tension? Anxiety asthma?

Gran Sophie continued to climb up here until her late eighties to sit and sketch valley scenes she would use for the oil paintings she did in the winter. She called this, "A spiritual place to meditate the seen and unseen." In 1911, after she received two watercolour paintings that her missionary sister Kate Fisher had done of the hills around Baalbek and Abeile, Jerusalem, she named this hill Camel Back. Because, she said, "Our Camel Back Hill has two humps like the beasts of burden in the Holy Land."

Once, many years ago when I was a young girl, after Mr. Martell finished digging a new hole for our biffy and I kept him company while he rolled and smoked a cigarette, he told me this rock was a teardrop left by his ancestors on the brow of the hill.

"So's the people that's strong an' not scared got a place to see in four directions," he said.

He pinched the paper at one end and licked his bottom lip so the lit cigarette would stick there while he talked.

"Them spirits speak loud, girl. Dreams'll come round. An' youse gotta be strong for it. Real strong."

I nodded as if I knew what he meant. We were sitting side by side in front of the mound of earth beside the new hole. I liked the slow way Mr. Martell talked, the silent spaces he left after each thing he said, and I liked the smell of his cigarette smoke mixed with the scent of the moist loam and clay behind us. Mr. Martell's arms reminded me of the dry branches that broke off our ash trees when the breeze was so light the poplars were just clapping their leaves politely. He didn't look strong enough to dig a six-foot hole. But people who ice-fished at Katepwa told how he often climbed to the Lookout Stone, quick as a deer, and sat here for hours, even if it was twenty below zero with a bad wind.

In the summers, I sat here a lot. I was the first one to see my father coming into the valley on Friday nights and the last to see him going out Sunday nights. Sometimes Mr. Martell came out of his house on the edge of No Man's Land down by the dam and raised his arm toward me in greeting. I waved back in a beckoning manner, but after a few moments he always lowered his arm and turned away.

Mr. Martell's two-storey clapboard house was hauled away years ago; his big vegetable garden was ploughed up and seeded with grass that the new property owner keeps shaved like a golf-green. The misspelled RUHBARB FOR SALE sign is gone. Modern city-style houses with landscaped yards line the shore of No Man's Land at the end of the lake down by the dam where the Laroche families used to live year-round in clusters of white-washed cabins. I miss the doleful baying of their coyote-mix mongrels.

Changes come and go in a circle around this rock. Bubbles of cactus, still covered with lace shrouds of last year's needles, are beginning new networks of sharp pointed barbs to spear the sun. Tiger lilies, roots warmed under the hill's scruffy hide, are ready to flame briefly like torches. Summer is starting its semi-circle of expected surprises. Nothing will happen for the last time, or for the first time, here, as it did on that Victoria Day weekend seven months after my father died.

Mother had promised we would open the cottage as usual – except she wanted to wait until Saturday morning to drive to the valley. Kenny and I packed the car for her on Friday night. We didn't fight. He called me "Sis" instead of "Fang Face" and I called him "Kid" instead of "Brat". We said, "Excuse me" to each other. Even Heather behaved nicely, skipping back and forth to the car carrying small things for us without whining. Everyone was cheerful. But long after we had some cocoa and said our good nights, I heard Mother crying softly again in bed.

She didn't do that often, only before *firsts*: Dad's forty-eighth birthday (nineteen days after his fatal coronary thrombosis); Christmas Eve; my eighteenth birthday in January; Valentine's night; and on a few nights when I didn't know what she was going to have to get through for the first time on her own. The sound of my mother's muffled sobs always made me cry too. When she stopped crying and I was finally able to fall asleep, I would dream my father was really still alive, but, for some reason he hadn't explained, it was a secret I had to keep.

In those dreams, I would wake up, go outside, and find my father in a garden of Qu'Appelle Valley plants he had moved to our backyard in Regina. When the dreams began before his birthday in November, I'd found him striding around making a pie in the snow. Later, when spring came and the snow melted in puddles frozen over with rubber ice, he was squishing through the wet crested wheat grass, stopping to inspect his plants and shrubs for the first signs of green shoots or buds. I walked beside him, circling the garden with him, not a bit cold in my pyjamas and bare feet. We talked about things that had happened since he'd gone away. It was just as if he had come back from a medical meeting in Winnipeg or Saskatoon and I was the first one to welcome him home. I kept forgetting to tell him Mother had been crying.

Everything went wrong in the dream I had that Friday night in May before we opened the cottage without him.

My father was sitting in a wheelchair with his back toward me when I came out of the house. He was outside of his garden, parked in front of the archway he'd built as an entrance into it. The back door slammed shut behind me, but the noise didn't attract his attention. It was very cold, so cold the step seemed to be iced, and my feet stuck to it as my tongue once had on the metal flagpole at school.

"Hi, Daddy. Dad? Hey! You're not going to try and get through that dumb arch in that stupid wheelchair, are you?" My voice got louder with each word, and gusts of wind whipped my frozen breath up to Mother's bedroom window, where each puff shattered against the glass like sleet. She would wake up and start crying again.

I lowered my voice to a stage whisper. "It's Victoria Day weekend, Dad, time to whistle while we work opening the cottage. Remember? What's going on?"

My father didn't move; didn't take his hands off the chair's wheels, didn't turn around or speak.

"It's all your fault," I said. "You can't get through to the garden sitting in that stupid thing." He'd built the tête-à-tête benches inside the trellis arch too close together. It was a family joke. He used to say the anatomy of benches in archways eluded him. I wanted to say something funny about how he had misread his own carefully drawn plans and hear him laugh about it again, but I just kept repeating, "Your fault, your fault. Fault. Fault."

"What?" he exclaimed. "What the hell's bells?"

He still didn't turn or (I was waiting for it) jump out of the wheelchair with a whoop to grab me and dance me through the arch – as if I was Ginger Rogers and he was Fred Astaire. We weren't going to trip the light fantastic around his dream garden to celebrate signs of summer.

"A good doctor wouldn't have done it," I yelled, and watched my words order themselves into a sign across the top of the archway. Each letter was formed of frozen droplets of spit that winked like tiny Christmas tree bulbs.

"What? What-what-what?" My father turned to face me. He was smiling the way he did when I forgot the punchline of a joke or couldn't solve one of his riddles.

The soles of my feet burned with pain as I pulled them off the iced back step and walked toward him. "Don't you mean, 'I beg your pardon,' Father?" I slid by him and went through the archway, hoping he would get out of the ugly chair and follow me. I circled his garden, dancing lightly on my toes from plant to plant, touching a budding branch or green shoot before pirouetting to the next one. He had been so careful transplanting each one from the valley loam to city gumbo – chokecherry and Saskatoon bushes, cactus, and, next to neatly labelled stakes, tiger lilies, brown-eyed Susans, wild snap dragons we called scrambled eggs, and a weed he was sure was going to turn out to be ditch daisies.

I spun back out through the archway like a dust devil and stopped in front of him. "Your garden's going to be a mess unless you stick around and show me how to look after it. Everything will die," I said.

"Yes," he said, "everything does. In the meantime, errors of commission are regarded with tolerance and understanding. Errors of omission are inexcusable."

"But you omitted to live!" I shouted.

Suddenly, his head lolled forward and his mouth sagged open. The flesh began melting off his face and drooling down his chin onto his chest.

"Stop it! Stop it!" I screamed. "You can't be like that. Not ever. Not dead. Dying. Stop joking. It's not funny." I knelt down and tried to shake the wheelchair, sobbing and saying, "Listen, Daddy, it's okay. It's okay if you're in a wheelchair. We don't care if you're crippled. Please Daddy, please stop it. Wake up, wake up, oh, please wake –"

I awoke from that dream hanging onto the cold radiator beside my bed, trying to shake it. Spittle was running down my chin. Something had gone wrong. I had awakened too soon. The dream wasn't over. It couldn't be. I had to go back to sleep, fix up the ending, wake up knowing I could coax him to come back in another dream and everything would be the same again. But I knew it was too late. Something had changed, ended.

Gradually, the view from this Lookout Stone has changed, like much in my life. The pit in the Little Lime Hill on the lakeside of the highway, where we dumped our tin cans and broken glass when I was a child, has long since been filled and sealed with cement as a pad to park the owners' cars. To the north, next to Camel Back on our property, Mother Bunting Hill has sagged so her nipple no longer seems to rub the sky. In front of her, the scars of motorcycles and snowmobiles on Baby Bunting Hill are ripe and raw in the sun. Now, poodles yip and big pedigreed dogs bark or whine behind locked screen patio doors and steel link fences too high to jump.

But if I look off to the south, beyond the end of the lake to the double arches of the cement bridge on the old road coming into the valley, no time has passed up here.

I can see Mother gripping the steering wheel of the new '49 Chevrolet as we reach the foot of Corkscrew Hill and approach the rickety cow bridge over Skinner's Creek. Her knuckles are white. Dad always patted the old Green Hornet's dashboard and then honked the horn when we made it safely across the bridge without it caving in. "You're a great old crate," he would say, winking at Mother. "I may never trade you in." But he'd made all the arrangements to replace the Hornet and died without ever driving the new Chevy into the valley.

Mother drove slowly, squinting into the morning sun. She'd cried a long time last night and her eyelids were pink and puffy. We didn't chant the usual refrain to celebrate the beginning of summer when we saw the lake, but I could hear the echo of our voices:

May the Twenty-fourth is
The Queen's birthday.
If we don't get a holiday,
We'll all run away.

Running away wasn't what we were doing. We crept along the valley road. And I knew Mother had been right to wait until daytime. Opening the cottage at night without him would have been worse. Darkness everywhere. Closed shutters. Padlocked doors. Only damp matches in a tin up on a shelf too high to reach to light the oil lamps and cookstove. Making our beds with flannelette slabs wintered in the black bedding box Dad had built. No. Kenny and I had known better than to even discuss it with Mother. This trip could only be almost the same, not exactly how it had been when Dad brought us down to open the cottage.

Mother stepped on the gas on the straight stretch of road before the cement bridge. The speedometer needle went up to the speed limit of forty-five.

Yes, I thought, let's get it over with.

Kenny dropped his *Batman* comic book on the back seat beside him and leaned forward, grinning. "You gonna honk the horn now, Mom? I'll show you how." He hit the back of the seat with his fist and said, "Honk! Honk! Honk-honk!"

"Hip! Hip! Hoo-ray!" Heather yelled, bouncing up on the seat between Mother and me to see how close we were to the cottage.

Heather was right. Dad's honking always sounded like a cheer, especially from up here on the Lookout Stone.

Mother honked, but it was different. It wasn't just the new car, a sleek grey ghost compared to the Green Hornet, the bitter smell of some car salesman's cigar smoke still caught in its upholstery. The rhythm was wrong. The sound was slow and heavy.

"So young – so young – so young," everyone said when my father died. That had sounded wrong to me then too. I thought it described someone like a boy I'd been secretly in love with who'd died when he was in grade eleven and I was in grade nine. He was buried just a few days before his sixteenth birthday, not his forty-eighth. I didn't think "so young" applied to my father. After all, I was nearly nineteen, an adult, and his hair was getting grey. But he was a doctor, and I just couldn't believe a doctor would let himself die.

At first it seemed dramatic and exciting when Uncle Wilf, my father's older brother, came to get me at Reliance Business School. The principal ushered him into the classroom in the middle of a shorthand exam she was giving us. I could see why my father called his older brother The Deacon and what he meant when he teased Uncle Wilf that he walked with his eyes cast heavenwards and didn't seem to approve of what he saw up there. Uncle Wilf put his hand on my shoulder, and said, "Your father is gravely ill, Pat." His voice was hushed, but everybody in the classroom heard him. "Your mother asked me to bring you home."

I got up and followed him down the aisle to the door. I left the exam papers and my stenographer's notebook on my desk.

A good secretary wouldn't leave a mess like that, I thought, I'll flunk shorthand and office deportment.

"Is my father sick enough to die?" I asked Uncle Wilf as soon as we were outside. I was recalling deathbed scenes in novels where family members stood around the dying person's bed, saying interesting things about life. I couldn't remember what. The favourite daughter usually vowed to fulfill some goal her dying parent had set for her. I wanted to tell my father I'd changed my mind and did want to go to university after all. But then I would have to keep my word and go. I stepped on Uncle Wilf's heels and asked again, "Is Daddy dying, Uncle Wilf?"

"Your father is gravely ill, Pat," he repeated, his voice hoarse. "We don't have any time to waste talking."

Our front door was never locked, but that day my uncle's wife, Aunt Lola, was there holding it open for us. I wondered why she wasn't upstairs with the others, around his bed, and then I remembered deathbed scenes usually end with someone really dying. But my aunt wrapped her arms around me as she usually did to greet me – except so tightly I could hardly breathe. I managed to struggle free, and ask, "Is Daddy okay?"

"He's fine now, darling, just fine." Aunt Lola sighed and patted my cheek.

That was when I started to shake. I ran through the vestibule, the front hall, and got halfway up the stairs to my parents' bedroom before I stumbled and had to sit down. He's just fine, I thought. Thank you, God. Everything is okay. How do you write "okay" in shorthand? I put my head down and sobbed with relief.

"Pat, oh, Pat. It's all right. Go ahead. Cry, dear." My mother was kneeling on the stairs in front of me, stroking my hair. "It was very quick, dear," she said. "He didn't suffer before he died."

"He died? Died?"

Mother hugged me.

"Is he dead?" I asked.

"Yes, dear," Mother answered softly.

I looked down at Aunt Lola, who was standing at the foot of the stairs hugging herself, her face all crinkled up, weeping tearlessly. Mother turned and looked at her too. "She's a liar," I said. "Why did she say Daddy was fine?" If Mother answered, I didn't hear her over my sobs.

I tried to avoid my aunt during the next few days. It wasn't easy. She was everywhere, serving sandwiches and dainties, coffee or tea, delivering drinks from Uncle Wilf's bar. She lived up to her reputation as the Queen City's perfect hostess, but I didn't see her smile once.

Mother seemed to be smiling all the time. She met people at the door with a smile, and she led the laughter after anecdotes they told about funny things my father had said or done on the golf course, at the poker table, and at medical meetings. Mother smiled when she told them my father liked to consider himself a natural born carpenter. She said he'd designed a secret compartment for the new library desk at the cancer clinic, and helped the cabinetmaker install it, so that nobody, including her, had been able to find it. A murmur of "so young" followed some of the stories, almost like a forgotten punchline. The unspoken words were there under my mother's tinkling laughter, and my aunt's sombre offerings of tea, coffee, or – said with her customary sigh – something stronger if she could find it. Scotch, rye whiskey and sherry were all out in plain view on the dining room buffet.

There wasn't any company for Mother to smile for before the funeral. We had the living room all to ourselves as we waited for the limousine to pick us up and take us to the church.

"You know what I'm going to do?" Heather asked. "I'm going to rap on the glass of Daddy's coffin and tell him to sing 'Cruising Down The River' with me."

Mother stopped pacing back and forth in front of her upholstered rocker that faced my father's empty easy chair, and sat down in it. "Well, we aren't going to sing that song today, dear," Mother said, motioning for Heather to get on her lap. She smiled. "It's a bit too cheerful, sweetheart. We'll sing 'Unto The Hills Beyond' instead. You'll like it too, Heather. It was one of your daddy's favourite psalms."

Kenny sat down in Dad's chair and crossed his legs. "His coffin's oak, anyway, not glass. Dad loved good wood. He said if he hadn't wanted to be a doctor, he would have been a carpenter."

"It's glass!" Heather screamed. "So shut up!"

"Hush, Heather. No it isn't. Kenny is right," Mother said. "What on earth gave you the idea it was glass?"

"Daddy said Snow White had a glass coffin," Heather said, and she began crying. She stopped when Mother laughed.

"Snow White? Snow White?" Mother laughed as she had when the visitors were there, in crescendos, the way she laughed at cocktail parties to fill awkward silences.

The same way we all laughed while we were opening the cottage that May. Kenny was so proud that he'd remembered to bring a pocketful of dry Eddy matches. One by one, he broke them, snapping the heads off as he tried to strike them on the seat of his pants to light the cookstove, the way Dad always did. Kenny started to cry, soundlessly, and ran out of the cottage. We just stood there, cold and shivering. The cottage was like a tomb. I went out to find Kenny and climbed up here to the Lookout Stone.

That time, I didn't sit down. I stood on this rock poised like an Olympic torchbearer. I was a statue, one foot ahead of the other in the footholds, my right arm held aloft, my hand a fist clenched around nothing. What was I thinking then? Citius, Altius, Fortius: Faster, Higher, Braver? Perhaps. I was proud of my B-plus in grade twelve Latin. I liked the idea of being able to translate a dead language into a living one.

I must have known the Olympic creed, too. The 1948 Games were one of my father's favourite topics in his last summer. Yes, I knew the creed: "Not to win, but to take part; not the triumph, but the struggle; not to have conquered, but to have fought well." But I didn't believe it, not then, standing on this stone with the last dream of my father circling away. I leapt off the Lookout Stone at a run, going faster and faster down the steep slope until I believed – I knew – that if the next step didn't split me in half, I would fly across the valley. I would soar to the top of Beacon Point Hill, and higher, higher. For one long stride, the valley was forgotten. My body and mind stretched up together and I was airborne before I fell. The scraping and tumbling ended in the wound where Camel Back's hide had been torn away to get at a vein of gravel.

I didn't move. I cursed my father for letting himself die, my aunt for the false hope she held out to me, and Mr. Martell too, for not teaching me to see in four directions.

Kenny found me lying there, my mouth full of sand, and we went back to the cottage together without speaking.

Now, I'm up here on the Lookout Stone, and, at the same time, I'm down on the grassy slope in front of our cottage, carrying things down from the new car, watching Kenny help Mother find the right keys for the padlocks. Heather is skipping back and forth singing "Cruising Down The River," getting in everyone's way. Mother is telling Kenny it's okay, she can open the cottage alone. We are all so young and scared down there opening the cottage for the first time without my father. I'm carrying his medical bag into the cold cottage, a nineteen-year-old dreamer who is telling herself it's the glare from the lake making her eyes water.

My vision is blurred as I look south toward the cement bridge with its curved arches, and I see my father coming into the valley. I hear the horn of the old Green Hornet: Hip! Hip! Hoo-ray!

And I wonder how a father who isn't quite forty-eight will greet a daughter so much older than he is now. What will we talk about? That he's so young to be dead? In his little black book, he wrote: *The greatest profession in the world is being a father.* Will we laugh or cry or be as silent as death?

Now, up here on the Lookout Stone, I'm not afraid. I look in four directions, gather spiritual strength, and pick my way carefully down the steep slope.

Torque

The rotational speed of seasons is dizzying since the October day I drove off the Chrysler lot in the only new car I've ever bought.

On a memory-go-round of cars I've owned, my white 1986 Plymouth Reliant station wagon alone belongs on the outer ring where the first carousel artisans enticed riders with their dreamiest horses. My dream on wheels had air, automatic locks and openers for the windows, hood, rear hatch, and gas tank lid. Plus, the gearshift up by the steering wheel and a front bench seat meant there was room beside me for my purse and two passengers. NLH on its new license plate provided the initials for its nickname: No Little Heap.

Leo, co-owner of the dealership, did the final inspection of NLH with Frank and me. We'd all gone to Central Collegiate in the Forties, but he and Frank were two years ahead of me.

Tall, dark and handsome, Leo still looked like Hollywood star Victor Mature in his prime. When Leo was in grade ten, Central's yearbook, *Ye Flame 1943*, said he "*Gets Edna to carry his books home.*" In grade eleven, he was described as: "*A wolf in the real sense of the word.*"

Abody Frank in grade nine, *Ye Flame* said: "*Noted for C-13.*" And, for a camera shy senior in grade twelve it said: "*In between designing cars and thinking up puns, Eyeball manages to squeeze in a little school work.*"

C-13 was Frank's number playing defence on Central's Golden Gophers senior hockey team. I could see in the *Ye Flame 1945* team photo that he needed a steady like me who would knit him a nightcap to flatten his elfin ears. When the Saturday matinee girls drooled over Perry Como in the musical, *Something For The Boys,* our Hedda Hopper said, "He's the silver screen image of silver blades C-13." We agreed being a star's look-alike meant act-alike and that Eyeball's relaxed amiable style was a real life version of Perry's, but sound-alike too? I knew if Eyeball ever crooned a love tune to me it would melt the moon.

Sound-alike act-alike applied to me. When my father was teaching me to drive, he said, "A smart young lady like you, with a voice like Lauren Bacall's, ought to act like a take-charge dame behind the wheel." He and Mother had just seen the movie *To Have And Have Not.* So had I. And I'd taken my turn leaning beside a cubicle door in the girl's washroom at Central, a piece of chalk held like a cigarette, saying in a smoky voice, "If you want anything, all you have to do is whistle."

At Leo's dealership, the impulse to wolf-whistle at my new limousine was hard to resist. NLH had charisma, pizzazz, oomph. Leo and Frank and I circled its gleaming body crowned by a chrome roof rack.

"Fair warning, Eyeball," Leo said as he and Frank looked in the half-open window on the driver's side. "That bench seat and shift stick will have zero appeal for resale to men."

"So...?" I bit my tongue.

Leo patted my shoulder and left his hand on it. Frank stepped to my other side and took my hand.

"Fine for the wife, though," Leo said. "Lots of room for kids and groceries. Good utility second car."

I shrugged off Leo's hand and took two giant steps forward, yanking Frank with me. His platinum ring that we'd given each other on our twenty-fifth wedding anniversary pressed against my little finger as I said, "Second? Is it a second-hand demonstrator?"

"Nope." Leo snorted and shook his head. "Hot to trot off the assembly line with lots of horsepower. No dung, like we said in our Central days. Want to look under the hood?"

"Nope, no, nay." I pulled my hand out of Frank's, and got in behind the wheel.

Frank smiled up at Leo, down at me, and said, "It's an SE K-car, custom-made for a gal with style and spunk."

"Yup," Leo said. "SE for Special Edition. K for the solid frame Chrysler invented to wipe out imported compacts."

"K for Krause," Frank said. "Not a yellow submarine, rock-and-roll jeep, souped-up '60s muscle car, or decor-van. It's a brand new sleek *patri*cian wagon that's all yours, hon."

I turned the key and the motor purred.

"Not four on the floor and buckets." Leo squatted, and the doppelgänger of the Samson-sized star billed as "a beautiful hunk of man," held his fist out by his right knee, made the sounds of an engine revving up and pretended to shift into overdrive.

I laughed. Hooted rudely, actually. Then I said, "Dames go for good looks plus utility and reliability. Maybe I'll get a vanity plate like my friend in Calgary has so the damn fools behind me

can see IBD BOSS, and eat my dust." I closed my window, shifted
to drive and took off, wondering if, perhaps, Leo had just
growled and pushed his fist forward in a go-for-it gesture.

So? Here I go: loving mom of three daughters and a son; fun
grandma; devoted wife of my star ex-Gopher and gofer; a working woman who's no damn fool. I've got a mile-wide smile on my
face, Madonna on the radio singing "Like A Virgin," and I'm a
liberated woman leaving on the paved driveway in front of the
showroom instead of the gravel road from Leo's used car lot. I
wave my hand in farewell to the old car nightmares and bad
scares I'd like to forget.

One car had a lighter that shot out red-hot and did an arc
into the back seat. I cried "Fire," slammed to a stop, evacuated
the kids, and retrieved it. That happened twice and I got rid of
the lighter. We sold the car without it and warned the buyer to
use a pocket lighter or matches if he smoked.

No more futile attempts to deodorize a car that smells of a
former owner's cigar smoke, cheap aftershave mixed with eye-
watering perfume, beer and vomit and diarrhea – all of which
survived industrial strength chemical cleansers and air sprays.
Who's crying now in a car that smells foul? Not me. I'm taking
deep breaths in a car that smells new, oh so fresh and new.

Stalled somewhere in the Seventies on the highway of my life,
there's a '58 Chevy sedan I inherited from Frank when he
bought his first new car. The gears locked in neutral at stoplights. My teenagers used to duck down or lie on the floor so
they wouldn't be seen in a car with the lady driver, often wearing a hat and white gloves, holding up traffic when the light
turned green. I had to turn off the engine, hop out, lift the
hood, manually turn the greasy teeth of the gearwheel, get back

in the car, restart the motor, back up a few feet in a blast of honking horns, brake, press the clutch and shift to low, and then hit the gas to go forward. Sometimes my youngest daughter disobeyed me and knelt on the back seat, looked out the rear window, and made faces at the driver behind us. Once, my eldest daughter got out of the car when it stalled and without looking back walked to our destination. My middle daughter usually clicked her tongue as if she was urging forward the horse she dreamed of getting. When my son's friends piled into the car to be driven somewhere, he said, "Car's old, so's my mom, but she's a grease monkey at stoplights and roars through the yellow like it's the Indy 500."

Now, sitting in the lap of luxury with my foot on the brake until the light is green and just pressing the gas to go forward makes me feel self-reliant. The motor hums a hymn to Chrysler's Lee Iacocca, who said the K-car "saved our bacon," and upped production. CBC Radio 540 is almost as static-free as CJME in this car and Hank Snow is singing "I'm Moving On."

The autumn sky is forget-me-not blue today, but a streak of clouds on the horizon has the winter flatness of torn flannel.

The first glitch in my dream car's performance happened on its virgin highway expedition. It was a bitterly cold December afternoon. Nine Regina family members were going to a wedding in Moose Jaw in two cars. We led the way. Frank had talked me into letting him test drive NLH on the highway. I was his front seat navigator-advisor. My mother, Florence, was in the back seat with our youngest daughter, Kathy, and her husband, Randy.

My sister Heather and her husband, John, were behind us in their '85 Honda Accord. Our eldest daughter Judy and her husband were in the back seat.

On road trips, Frank and Mother liked to exchange "*auto* biographies" about the cars they'd driven. They barely got started when No Little Heap began to hiccup as we approached the gas and snack stop outside the hamlet of Belle Plaine.

"Power light's blinking," I said. The hiccups got worse.

"What the heck?" Frank said, and the motor died. We coasted up to the gas pump and Frank braked to a stop.

Mother snapped open her purse. "Let me pay for the gas, Frank," she said. "It's the least I can do."

"We're not out of gas, Florence," Frank said. He tried to restart the car and nothing happened. It didn't even growl.

"Crank it, Frank," Mother said. "Pull out the choke and tramp down on the gas."

The Honda pulled in behind us. Two men in parkas and flapping seven league boots came out of the little snack shop. Everyone got out of the cars and milled around Frank and the two Belle Plaine men, peering in at the dead engine.

"Pat knows how to unlock gears," Mother said proudly. "I've been with her at stoplights and she did it quick as a wink. You get in there and show them, dear," she said, and gave me her no-nonsense nudge in the back with her cane.

Frozen gas line? Dead battery? Loose wire? Fan belt? Antifreeze? Oil leak? Overheated? It was question chaos. No answers. Nothing worked. Time was running out.

We decided to have my car towed to Leo's dealership and we would all go to Moose Jaw wedged in the Honda.

Mother's voice was muffled when she said, "Remember when

it was popular to see how many people could cram into a Volkswagen, Frank? Wasn't the record double this many? Guess they weren't wearing winter coats. It feels as if we're in a *Dinky Toy*."

NLH got a clean bill of health after its physical at the dealership. On Mother's 85th birthday, February 2, 1987, after the family brunch at the Hotel Saskatchewan, Frank and I took her on a Sunday drive in NLH. Frank suggested I should do a highway torque test by driving out to Balgonie. On the way back to the city the engine hiccupped a few times and the power loss light flickered.

"Is your car still a bit colicky, dear? Do you want me to take over and drive for a while?" Mother undid her seat belt.

"Fasten-up, Florence," Frank said. "It's okay."

Early Monday morning, Frank took my car back to Leo's mechanic and went over its chronic symptoms with him. Two days later, my car was ready to come home. The system diagnostics report had check marks beside functions even Frank didn't know it had. Above the head mechanic's signature on the report, in large block letters, was printed: GOOD AS NEW!

"Well, law-tee-dah," I said when Frank showed me. "It's only four months old."

"Maybe Florence was right and it was colic, " Frank said.

The highway rodeo rides began again in the middle of May when we started going to and from the cottage. Frank and I, Mother and her pal Scottie, our cute little Terripoo mutt, made two nerve-wracking round trips. Sometimes Frank was driving and sometimes I was when the bucking started, then the power loss light flickered warning the driver to get over on the shoulder before the motor died. During the forced engine-rest stops,

Mother stroked Scottie and told him stories about family pets that had spent idyllic summers at the lake from 1905 onward. It was just a hop, skip and jump through eight decades of summer memories for her to remember the names and idiosyncrasies of a menagerie of creatures including a garter snake named Slither that rose up on its tail and swayed to tunes she played on a comb with tissue paper wrapped around it.

In June, the exciting month of weekends when summer lies stretched out ahead, the Reliant spent more time in Leo's garage with its hood raised or its body up on the hoist than under the roof of our Regina carport or the ash trees at the lake.

That month I renamed the car New Lemon Horror and Mother told me to enunciate the final syllable more clearly so it didn't sound like its last name was Whore. Mother had given up driving after 69 years and missed wheeling about in her '74 Dodge Dart Frank helped her buy. She was mourning the end of her driving life freedom, and her own loss of power made her edgy. She wished she'd just put her car up on winter blocks and not made such a snap decision to sell it. She repeatedly said, "I could have loaned my Dart to you indefinitely while you wait for Leo to fix your balky station wagon."

Long-distance phone calls Frank made to Chrysler's head office in Winnipeg weren't returned. His letters got no replies, not even the one he sent registered mail. I told him to quit being so relaxed and amiable, to take his hands out of his cardigan pockets, put up his fists, and force that Samson-size rip-off star Leo *Manure* to make Chrysler fix my damn car or give me a new one. No love tunes were crooned in bed that night.

Mother and Scottie and I drove out to the cottage in NLH without a problem at the end of June and stayed there. Frank came for weekends and so did hordes of family and friends. On Monday, July 27, the day after Heather's forty-seventh birthday, a multitude of weekenders and party guests left us with mounds of towels and sheets that had to be washed before the next onslaught. The heat wave made us decide to bypass the coin laundry in Indian Head, which wasn't air-conditioned, and drive home to Regina. We left at 7:30 a.m., expecting to arrive cool and collected an hour later. The bucking car and its four power shutdowns caused us to sweat it out at the side of the highway for a total of two hours. It was too hot to talk without air-conditioning. Mother said, "Hell's bells," several times, and claimed she heard them ringing. Each time the car bucked and the motor died, the way she growled "Chrys-ler" sounded blasphemous.

At 10:33 a.m., my tongue too dry to wag, I pulled into our driveway. It took me ten minutes to get Mother and Scottie settled inside our air-conditioned house and carry in the dirty laundry. I wheeled into Leo's dealership lot at 10:53, switched off the motor, and marched across the showroom floor to the sales desk where a couple of salesmen were lounging. They watched me approach. They did not mistake me for a satisfied customer. I slammed my car keys down on the curved counter, and said, "I want to see the owner right now. It's an emergency."

Both men kept smiling a wolfish come-on. The one in the pink short-sleeved shirt said, "Leo's not here. He's in court."

I said, "Good! He should get used to it because that's where I'm taking him if he doesn't fix my car and give me a new one to drive until he does. Who's in charge here?"

There was some muttering and mumbling. I leaned over and put my fists on the counter. The salesman in the checked sports jacket called the sales manager to come and speak to me. He got an earful. I said, "My frail eighty-five-year-old mother and Terripoo are limp and sick with heat exhaustion and might die of heat stroke after riding in that lemon Leo sold me. It took three hellish hours to get from Katepwa to Regina. That new Plymouth so-called *utility* vehicle sitting out there in your driveway almost made us roadkill. It lost its power four damn times. I had to pull over to the side of the busy highway, and my elderly mother and dog and I had to sit in the stifling heat with a load of dirty laundry. I want a new four-door car to drive – with air and a bench seat in front that has room for my purse and my mother's purse and my watchdog to sit up on, because I'll sue Leo, no dung, unless he fixes that horror or makes Chrysler recall it and give me a new car."

The manager gave me the keys to a new '87 baby blue four-door Le Baron sedan with air. The only things it had that I didn't want were bucket seats and four on the floor.

I drove Mother and Scottie and the stacks of neatly folded fresh-smelling laundry back to Katepwa, and Leo's royal Le Baron hummed along at 100K without a gurgle.

During the early part of the week, it's usually quiet enough at the cottage to read, write, and think. In preparation for a possible court case, I drafted a letter to Leo outlining my complaint:

I will swear in court under oath that my 1986 Plymouth Reliant has bucked like a bronco at highway speeds and lost power ever since the first time we took it out of town on a cold December day ten weeks after I bought it. This is not something I have imagined. Frank and I, my eighty-five-year-old mother and our dog all have saddle sores on our nerves to prove it.

I would like to have the following things certified in writing before accepting the fact that we are stuck with a lemon and nothing can be done to correct this serious problem:

1) A list of possible things that could cause this chronic problem and which ones you have checked and found to be in 100% working order since you received the car at 10:55 am, Monday, July 27.

2) Confirmation that the car was driven 140 kilometres at highway speeds of 100 K by your experts and did not buck or have the power loss light come on.

3) Why you believe the problem only occurs when Frank or I drive this car on the highway.

4) Your explanation for why the car has continued to buck and lose power at highway speeds ever since we bought it, but does not act up in the city at 50 K or lower – or ever when your people test it.

5) Your recommendations as to what we should do when the car starts to buck on the highway to prevent the loss of power.

6) A guarantee from you (over your dated and notarized signature) that this car is safe to drive on the highway in its present condition.

Since May of this year, trips to and from Lake Katepwa have been a nightmare of violent bucking and power losses. I am not willing to put up with this dangerous situation any longer. Diddling around changing spark plugs and making other minor adjustments have proven to be a waste of time and money for Chrysler and for us. If you are unable (or unwilling) to do whatever is necessary to fix this car without further expense to us so it is safe on the highway, please state that in writing.

Mother read it, and said, "Oh, I don't know, dear. It's a good letter, but –"

"But what?"

"Well, why don't you just keep the cute baby blue Le Baron? I like having that hump in the front between us with places to put our coffee cups, and Scottie likes lying on the floor with his nose at the air-conditioner vent."

Instead of mailing the letter to Leo, I phoned Frank's cousin, a recently appointed Queen's Counsel, read him the letter, and asked if he would be my lawyer.

He said, "Doesn't sound like you need one, Pat, but go ahead and tell Leo to contact me. I had a court case against him Monday and won a large settlement from him for my client."

On Friday, Leo phoned to say I'd be glad to know my car was gung-ho to go. They'd fixed a malfunction in its computerized power system, tested it on the highway twice, and it was running like greased lightning. I could bring back his Le Baron and pick it up. I said, no, that wouldn't be convenient. Why didn't he send it out to me at Katepwa? That would give it a third highway test just to be sure. He said he couldn't afford to take someone off the job and pay overtime to deliver a car that far. Then he tried some crass flattery by lowering his voice to a Rolls Royce murmur and saying I was his favourite "whistle-bait starlet" when we were in Central together. I reminded him he was halfway through high school when I started and years older. I asked why he didn't tell one of his guys he'd pay the dinner bill for two at the Katepwa Hotel. He could take his wife or girlfriend on a date to the Qu'Appelle Valley and drive back to town in a luxurious Le Baron. Leo said none of the guys would go for that. I said that was because a couple can't cuddle in bucket seats. Back seat's a couch, Leo said. He said to call him back and let him know what time I'd be there to return his Le Baron and pick up my wagon.

I didn't phone him.

Twenty minutes later, Leo called back to say one of his guys was going to run my car out to me in the late afternoon.

It was a thrill to see my handsome white station wagon coming down the trail to the cottage. I went out with the keys to Leo's Le Baron. A man and a woman got out of my car. I was glad to hear they hadn't had any power loss problems and asked if they were heading right back to Regina. The man grinned and said the boss gave him his Visa to take his wife to dinner at the hotel. I said the beef wellington was excellent.

When Frank arrived at 6 p.m., Mother and Scottie and I were cooling off in No Little Heap with the air on high and the radio on low. Scottie had a bowl of water and a rawhide bone; Mother and I had gin and tonics. Frank got a cold beer and stretched out on the back seat with Scottie.

"Good thing I took NLH to a computer diagnostic shop and the technician identified the faulty code," Frank said. "It was a cinch to fix once Leo's mechanic had the diagram. Could have done it myself."

It took a minute for that to sink in. I said, "*You* found out what was wrong?"

Mother said, "Good for you, Frank. Here's to a son-in-law who knows his cars inside out," and took a sip of her gin and tonic.

I said, "Wow! Here's to my guy Eye, a man for all seasons."

We all raised our glasses and toasted each other, No Little Heap, torque, and life in the fast lane. Scottie made the rounds jumping up to lick our faces.

But what made it a pluperfect tailgate party was Perry Como on the radio singing, "Hoop-Dee-Doo."

Sunburst

March 23, 1992

Spring is an imaginary season in Saskatchewan, and I wish Frank and I were all set to fly to Florida for the real thing. But it wasn't meant to be this year. We'll have to get by with our '91 memories of April in Sarasota and our quick round trip there in November when we stayed at St. Pete's beach for an airline reunion.

We defined *reunion* as the harmonious act of coming together again in a warm climate.

As Frank said when we were packing, "Almost a week of heat in a November cold snap is nothing to sneeze at."

I faked a sneeze. So did he.

"Gesundheit!" he said. "Hot nights are good for tickles so let's pack like moonlight nudists."

We have an ironclad rule to pack only the bare necessities and take at least one item out before closing the suitcase. Our rule was made in the days we took our four children to Europe on airline passes and packed everything we needed in two suitcases. Two bags full is a balanced load, Frank said as he led us on the long trek up the stairs, climbing high to the cheapest rooms in our pension. It's a wonder we didn't have nosebleeds. Now, in our sunset years when it's either the main floor or an elevator, Frank and I each take a carry-on and a weekender bag on wheels. Bulky things we won't leave home without go on board in the carry-on. My laptop computer and Adidas to speed-shop go in my quilted nylon JETBAG with padded shoulder straps. In his attaché case Frank carries his Canon camera and the astronaut binoculars he uses to try and see the fabled lucky green flash as the last rim of sun disappears in the Gulf.

The reunion we went to was for people who worked for Air Canada when it was Trans-Canada Air Lines – TCA for short. Most of the TCA old-timers come in groups from Montreal and Toronto. Like Frank, they're members of a TCA/AC family of devoted loyalists who enjoyed lifetime careers with the airline. Privatizing, open skies, competing and downsizing are the business buzz saws cutting down the family tree. Employees are "laid off" (today's euphemism for fired) before they've been on the payroll long enough to earn their wings, or forced to retire in mid-career with tin-cup pensions. At a recent retirement party we were at in Regina, one reluctant retiree in his forties with fifteen years service told the bitter truth. In his thank-you-for-the-piece-of-luggage speech, he said that instead of the old-fashioned gold watch, he'd gotten the newfangled platinum finger. Frank laughed, but he doesn't usually take kindly to even gentle criticisms of his airline. Just joking around saying that Tin Can Airlines became Air Can-a-duh then Air Cash is a major mistake if you value his friendship.

More than once, we've been the only couple at the reunion from Saskatchewan, but last November the two men who preceded Frank as Saskatchewan managers were there with their wives.

Jack and his second wife, Margaret, who is also a TCA/AC retiree, came all the way from Delta, British Columbia. Jack, who turned eighty-five the day of the banquet, is still spry enough to jump over the candelabra on a grand piano thanks to Margaret's loving care and companionship. Jack hired Frank in 1950. At that time, Margaret, a thirtysomething single woman who lived with and cared for her elderly parents, was Jack's efficient and protective secretary.

I've been thinking about Jack's first wife, Gladys, lately. Everyone called her Glad because of her perky personality and friendliness. She and Jack often invited the TCA staff to their home for dinner parties and singalongs with Jack playing favourite songs on the piano. In the early Fifties, Glad was diagnosed with breast cancer. For over five years, she was a "responder" who bounced back from every recurrence after treatment, until the last experimental surgery to remove her thymus gland. Frank and I went to see her when she was literally on her deathbed. She was at home and Jack was looking after her. He let us in and took us upstairs to their bedroom. Glad lived up to her name greeting us. She wasn't wearing her wig. A wisp of her hair was brushed up in a curl on top of her head like a baby girl's and tied with pink ribbon. She chatted with us about our children's activities and what we were busy doing. The only sign she was in pain was the way she kept moving one leg back and forth under the covers like a pendulum.

After Glad's death, Jack was given the option of retiring early or going to Australia, to open a TCA sales office. He chose the transfer, married Margaret, and finished his career down under.

Bob, Jack's successor and the district manager Frank replaced, and his wife, Mary, came from Regina on a different flight than ours. So we had a Saskatchewan table of six for cocktails, dinners and dances that featured taped music of the forties, fifties and sixties that made the old and zestless feel like the young and restless. We should have knocked on wood. There's an airline joke about a customer who calls a Reservations 800-number and asks for a return ticket. "Where to?" the agent asks. "Back here, of course," the customer replies. Like the music, many things reminded us of when we were young and agile. The return to a past "Here" was disembodied.

Our room at the Breckenridge had a sleek modern wall-bed between glossy white bookcases and bedside tables. The bed glided down with a feather-light touch. We tested the comfort of its box spring and smooth foam mattress before putting on our casual Florida clothes and going downstairs to register for the reunion.

"Sure isn't like that creaky Murphy and prickly horsehair mattress we had as newlyweds," Frank said afterwards. "It's as lush as being in the back seat of a parked Jaguar."

"With whom?" I asked.

"The girl with the *joie de vivre* to test it with me, of course," he said, and gave me a good long French kiss.

We did another test before the cash-bar mixer and welcoming dinner, and tried to accomplish a third after our nightcaps.

Frank said, "This is going to take some getting used to, but we've got five more nights."

"And days," I said, and we went to sleep.

Before dawn Saturday morning a horrible sound woke me up. I sat bolt upright. It took me a moment to realize the noise was Frank throwing up so violently it scared me. He wouldn't let me come in the bathroom to help. He yelled at me to shut the door, but before I did I saw that what he was vomiting into the toilet was blood red. It was daylight by the time the rasp of his dry heaves stopped. Then, he cleaned up the bathroom, washed his pyjama top in the tub, had a shower and came out in a towel sarong to lie down on the bed.

We blamed his ordeal on the extra spicy *Yankee Doodle Dandy* tomato juice we'd used as Bloody Mary mix in drinks to celebrate our arrival and in our nightcaps.

I said, "That damn Yankee mix didn't agree with me either, and I like spicy things."

Frank said, "A sweet li'l Alabama-born gal who says damn Yankee like one word ought've brought along Mott's for her good ole boy."

On Saturday afternoon, when Mary let go of Bob's arm to whip across the street to a new boutique having an opening sale, she slipped on a palm leaf and fell. She had trouble getting up and pain walking. Bob had to wave the traffic around them until he was able to stop a taxi and take her to the hospital. Neither Bob nor Jack had rented a car. Retired from hassle, they said. They'd used different vans from Tampa Airport to the hotel, and both of their young drivers had told their passengers about a couple in their seventies who made a wrong turn going by St. Petersburg Airport and drove down the main runway, over the low seawall at the end of it, and into the Gulf. Fortunately, the couple weren't hurt and their Mercedes-Benz looked as if it was just testing the temperature of the water with its nose. True or not, the story was the hit of the airline reunion and was embellished every time it was told.

Jack remembered his driver saying the old guy at the wheel kept shaking his head and repeating, "I told her a Florida freeway without any traffic only exists in dreamland." That triggered Bob's memory of his driver saying the old lady just sat there crocheting a stars and stripes afghan and smiling down at her speeding hand wielding the hook.

Frank volunteered to run a shuttle service to the hospital Mary was in overnight with a badly twisted leg. Although Frank still had stomach cramps if he ate anything solid, he took Bob to visit Mary three times and the rest of us in shifts in the passenger seat of the racy red Camaro we'd rented.

On Tuesday, November 11, Veterans Day in the States, our Remembrance Day, and the date of my father's funeral in 1948, I had the homesick blues. At home on November 11th, we always take my mother for a drive wherever she wants to go. On a nice sunny day, it's to the cemetery in Indian Head to tidy up around my father's grave, then down to the Qu'Appelle Valley to see what it's like at our summer cottage with all the leaves gone. I had my laptop on to update my daily trip diary and watched the blue letters appear on its liquid crystal screen as I typed: *Early winter there, late summer here –*

Frank put his hands on my shoulders, and said, "Hey, hon, I'm feeling okay today so let's drive down to Sarasota and see if Eileen found us another condo for next April."

We'd expected to spend a fourth April in Dr. Russanow's condo, but his January-to-the-end-of-March renters had booked it until April 30th for '92. We were hoping there would be a rental in the building overlooking the inland waterway so Frank could use his binoculars on the porch for a close-up look at the birds and the show-off dolphins in the boat channel. Natalie and Milton would be neighbours and we could go over to Siesta Key's lookout to watch the sunset with them. Milton had become a green flash expert since they'd retired to Sarasota from Queens, New York. He said the scientific explanation for the green flash is that the instant the sun sinks below the horizon of the Gulf, there's a scattering and refraction of light beams. The sun's rays are bent and the last colour of light that flashes through the atmosphere with enough intensity to be seen is green. A clear cloudless sky at sundown was essential. So far, with only two nights left at St. Pete's, Frank hadn't had any luck sighting it – or getting rid of his stomach ache either.

We stopped at Gulf Gate Mall on the way to the condo office and shared a soup and sandwich lunch at Friday's. Then we slow-shopped at good old Terry Schulman's. I bought a blue papier-mâché pelican with a lid on its back over an empty belly big enough to hide love letters in if I can nag Frank into writing me some. I talked Frank into buying a yellow slicker to wear at home on rainy mornings when he walks four miles around Wascana Park with his brother Stan. It's called a JAC IN THE SAC MIGHTY-MAC. Frank followed the illustrated instructions inside one pocket and carried it out to the car in its own travel sack.

The condo office was closed and we walked around the complex a bit. Everything was as green and growing and clean as it was in April. Must be nice living in paradise year-round.

On our way back to St. Pete's, we took a detour over to St. Armand's Circle and drove around it twice. Frank parked across from Jacobsons and I took photos of him at the wheel of the red Camaro he fell madly in love with at first sight. He posed with his arm on the open window, smiling ear-to-ear. He's wearing his white T-shirt with wide red horizontal stripes and looks like a muscle car racer who just won the World Cup. Under the photo in our Florida album, he printed:

Pat to Camaro: You're too conceited about your beauty.
Camaro to Pat: Not at all. I don't think I'm half as good
looking as I am. Ask Eyeball.

That scarlet vamp purred all the way back to St. Pete's, but I was the one who stroked Frank's back with my fingertips to relieve his cramps. They were getting more frequent and severe. He couldn't eat a proper meal. New England clam chowder, a handful of those little round oyster crackers or a few soda crackers, bottled water and skim milk were the only things he could eat or drink that didn't double him over in pain. By restricting himself to what others told us was an ultra-ulcer diet, he was able to attend reunion functions and – between bathroom breaks to urinate – actually enjoy them. I know it wasn't easy for him to watch me sip goblets of wine and tuck away gourmet food at the seven-course banquet at which he only had the chilled consommé.

In spite of not eating, he had a miserable trip home. The romance of flight is long gone. It's hard work to travel by air these days – or am I just getting older and crankier? No, I don't think so. That doesn't change the facts. Cattle Class on a jumbo jet is tough if you're feeling well. Home in your own bed is where you want to be if you're sick.

We went to Tampa Airport five hours before our scheduled departure to select seats close to a washroom, and near an exit to help us make our tight connection for Regina in Toronto. On the flight down to Tampa, we were in Seats 402 and 403 and it took us twenty-five minutes to deplane. Going home, we had to clear Customs and run from one end of Pearson Airport to the other to catch our flight. To make matters worse, the Tampa/Toronto flight is often late arriving at Pearson, as it was that Thursday evening. Did that add to our anxiety? Let me count the ways. Almost stationary mile-long queues at Customs, the mad scramble through a milling mob up to departure level, a clog at security, and the marathon to the boarding gate to check in before our flight left. I knew from Frank's pinched look and damp face that he felt rotten. Once we were on the plane, runway congestion meant we waited in line to take off for over an hour before we even began our three-hour flight home.

We didn't hold hands for takeoff because Frank was turned away from me asleep. He had the window seat, I was in the middle seat, and a woman with a shrill magpie voice was in the aisle seat. As soon as we were settled, and Frank had laid his head on the pillow he got from the overhead bin and put against the window, she used her beak to make ice pick stabs of words on my eardrum.

"That your husband? He's a handsome fellow. Looks awful sick. Man I got hitched to near fifty years ago was homely in looks..."

I'd bought a book on the bestsellers' table at a bookstore in Tampa Airport and I wanted to read it. I *longed* to read *Dare To Be A Great Writer* by Leonard Bishop and memorize his *329 Keys To Powerful Fiction* that the subtitle promised were inside.

"Had a head hard and bald as a curling rock. Rubbed it like he'd raise a thought worth having. Is that a wig your hubby's got on?"

I said, "No, it isn't."

"Looks real," she said. "Bet there's a heap of warm thoughts under that snowdrift. Guess he don't want to mess it up, way he's sleeping. Does he wear a hairnet to bed at home?"

Frank groaned. I frowned at her and shook my head.
She sharpened her voice. "Is he a homebody man? Mine never was from day one. Off hiding somewheres all the time. Lost him for good last November. Didn't look much worse than your hubby before I lost him, neither." She leaned forward and turned her head so her face was in front of mine, and either smiled or grimaced. She looked more like the mythical ugly mugwump than a stately magpie.

I looked down at my book, unopened. The last thing I wanted was for my silence to work like it used to when I did radio interviews and got stuck with someone who just nodded and shook their head. Five or six seconds of dead air caused a mute person to fill it with so many words I couldn't squeeze another question in sideways.

The question I wanted to ask the mugwump was based on one my newly widowed mother used to ask after she closed the door behind someone who'd said it was sad she'd lost her husband.

"Lost?" Mother asked the doorknob. "Like a mitt off a string? Why wouldn't I look till I found him? Lost is not dead."

I wanted to ask: Did you tell him to get lost because he was so homely? Have you looked in a mirror to find his double? Then I wanted to prop my book open on her jutting chin and read.

We got home so late, after midnight, Frank fell into bed and didn't call our doctor and arrange to meet him at Emergency until early Friday morning. Some blood tests were done and Frank was immediately admitted to the hospital. He was so anaemic they suspected he had serious internal bleeding and did a CAT scan with a surgeon standing by to operate in case he had an aneurysm. When nothing showed up in the CAT scan, they fed him on IV and did three days of all those awful tests on the poor guy that are either up-the-bottom or down-the-throat. He needed a blood transfusion, but they couldn't give him blood until some of the tests were completed because it could screw-up the results.

When those tests were done and showed nothing amiss, he received three bags of blood and, in addition to his IV, he was allowed to have clear fluids such as apple juice and fruit-flavoured gelatine desserts. Frank sang, "J-E-L-L-O," and said a bowl of green jelly never looked so good. The last test they did was the most uncomfortable. The examination of his digestive organs was done with a tiny camera attached to the end of a flexible tube of a surprisingly large diameter that was put down his throat to take pictures of his alimentary canal from top to bottom. It's fairly rare to have a tumour in the small intestine, but that's where Frank had one. He had surgery the next morning, Thursday, November 20th, a week after we got home. They took out the tumour along with three feet of his approximately twenty-two feet of small intestine to make sure if the biopsy showed the tumour was malignant no cancer cells were left behind to spread to his liver, spleen, or other vital organs.

Because Frank was in very good health before his sudden illness, and was physically fit from walking every weekday and keeping the lawns and gardens in tip-top shape at home in Regina and at the lake cottage, his recovery from the surgery was remarkably fast. He made his first witty remark before the anaesthetic had completely worn off. To appreciate it, you have to know something about the constitutional crisis drummed up by Prime Minister Mulroney and his political cohorts to keep our minds off the sad state of our economy. Most Canadians fall into a coma just hearing the word *constitution* in a newscast. Joe Clark, who was prime minister of Canada for a Saskatchewan second before losing the Progressive Conservative party leadership to Mulroney, was touring the country attempting to get a consensus of what the ROC (Rest Of Canada) was willing to give Quebec to keep it from separating. That's my background rant.

When the nurses brought Frank up from the Recovery Room and were moving him off the gurney onto the bed, he said, "If Joe Clark comes to see me, tell him to get lost."

Both nurses laughed and one of them said, "Yes sir! We'll tell any politicians who come to see you to get lost."

The thin handsome man in a snazzy business suit who came into the room two days later didn't look like any politician I'd seen in person or on TV. He strolled over to the foot of the bed as if he was a professional model or dancer and began asking Frank about how his bowels and bladder were functioning. Before Frank could describe the size, colour and texture of his feces, I interrupted, and said, "Wait a minute, who are you?" He introduced himself as one of the assisting surgeons and I changed the subject.

I said, "Tell me, during Frank's operation did the surgical team solve the constitutional crisis?"

He looked at me as if he'd held out his hand and snapped, "Scalpel," and I'd punctured his palm with the prongs of a fork.

I smiled, and said, "I've read there's evidence some people under anaesthetic hear every word of what's being discussed in the operating theatre."

He said, "Oh?"

I nodded my head ever so slightly.

"Of course, testimonials aren't scientific. But, yes, it's possible the subconscious isn't rendered insensible to sounds familiar to a patient." He smiled, slightly. "Such as political debates in this province."

"And words like constitution? Or names like Joe Clark?" I asked rhetorically.

We three smiled knowingly at each other: surgeon, patient, wife. "This happy ending is, pardon the pun, good for my constitution," Frank said.

The head surgeon came to see Frank late on the fourth post-operative day. After a pleasant how-are-you-feeling question, he got right to the point.

"The biopsy shows the tumour was cancerous," he said.

"How long have I got?" Frank asked.

That exchange was a one-two blow to my gut.

The surgeon answered unasked questions: "Caught early; got it all; four-week recovery; cancer clinic checkup; medication and exercise your family doctor will prescribe to build up your strength, and you'll be ready to boogie again, Mr. Krause."

Boogie? It reminded me how surprised I was when I first met the young surgeon and realized he wasn't the doctor I'd thought was going to operate; he was his son – the cute blond kid who'd hung around with our kids at Katepwa in the summer.

Frank smiled, and said, "Okay, no set death date. You wielded the knife and I have my life to schedule so I'll get my rhythm back to boogie-woogie again."

Now, to zap any cancer cells that might be lurking around undetected, Frank is more than halfway through a six-month program of chemotherapy at the cancer clinic named in memory of my father. It's a strange feeling to go to the Allan Blair Cancer

Centre with my husband. My father died two years before we were married. Frank and the other patients have their chemo in a big area that was once my father's office and the adjoining library. There was a built-in desk in the library with a secret drawer in it. My father used to boast he'd conspired with the cabinetmaker to craft a drawer so well hidden that even Edgar Allan Poe couldn't have solved the puzzle of its location. My mother and brother and I couldn't find it and neither could the clinic staff. I was sure there was a formula in it my father hadn't finished for the cure for cancer. If I'd known the desk was being sold at a public auction ten years ago when the clinic was remodelled, I would have bought it at any price. Frank sits in one of the La-Z-Boy chairs all hooked-up to tubes for chemo. A few badly stricken patients have to lie on gurneys.

I keep expecting to see my father's clinic motto on the wall somewhere. In the forties, when he was director of the clinic and of cancer services for the province, a nurse did it for him in cross-stitch. He said it added exactly the right homey touch to the art and science of giving good medical care.

> In this clinic....
> To be thorough, to be exact, to be painstaking
> and to be right, will bring no special praise.
> Errors of commission will be regarded with
> tolerance and understanding, but errors of
> omission will be considered inexcusable.
> – ALLAN WALKER BLAIR

That still seems to be the clinic motto judging from the excellent care Frank is receiving. Once a month – April 10th is the next time – Frank has a blood test, a physical, and then three and a half hours of chemo. He also goes to our family doctor once a month for a B-12 shot. He was told he would probably need the shots for the rest of his life, but our doctor says his blood is coming up so well he may be able to do without them after he finishes chemo. He's lucky it hasn't made him sick or caused him to lose his hair. He admits to being a bit weak and dozing off more often reading or watching TV or listening to me. He sure doesn't want me to treat him like an invalid. No babying – just adult cuddling and kissing and petting – plus physical activity to increase his heart rate as the doctor ordered. Sometimes Frank calls me princess, but I never ask, royally, "How are *we* feeling today?" He would answer like a grateful Canadian commoner. So will I.

We feel damn lucky to live in a country with *free* tax-paid health care. A short rundown of the highest costs includes: all the diagnostic tests, especially the CAT scan and two bone marrow aspirations; four hours of surgery; an anaesthetist; ten days in hospital; a special duty night nurse, and every test known in oncology.

We feel gratitude to people we'll never meet who stand on guard for the all-for-one Canada. Saskatchewan led the way to national tax-paid cancer treatment after the CCF (Cooperative Commonwealth Federation) won our 1944 provincial election and Premier Tommy Douglas made it a government program. The goal was to provide cancer care second to none in the world. My father asked for and got: bursaries for staff members to go and study at top institutions; higher salaries; money to buy the latest technical equipment; and attached to the then Grey Nuns Hospital, a new Regina cancer clinic building with a solarium on the roof for patients to use.

There's a photo of my father speaking at the opening ceremony of the new building in June 1948. He's standing at the microphone speaking, his hands hitched by his thumbs in the pockets of his suit jacket. Premier Douglas is sitting by his left side looking up at him attentively. Government dignitaries and Sister Superior backed by a flock of Grey Nuns are with the Premier on the outdoor stage.

Mother edited his notes for the speech and was there to hear him deliver it. She recalled for me how he emphasized the words he'd underlined: I _dedicate_ myself, and medical _people_ who work with me in this _grand_ new building, to _healing_ people with cancer, to _learning_ how to _eradicate_ cancer, and to leaving this building as empty of _patients_ as it is today waiting for us to get _started_.

Frank's last treatment will be in May so we'll stay close to home, the clinic, his oncologist and our family doctor until then. Frank is confident he'll be as good as new afterwards. He booked our flights and registered us for the Air Canada Pionairs Annual General Meeting in San Francisco that's being held a week after his last treatment.

I didn't get around to sending any season greeting cards last December. If I had, I would have been able to report that on December 18, less than a month after his operation, Frank was up on a stepladder in the bushes beside our carport stringing Christmas lights on the lilacs.

Saturday, June 28, 2003
Frank watched quite a few sunsets when we were in St. Pete's, hoping to see the lucky green flash. The window of our sixth-floor room at the Breckenridge faced west over the gulf.

Frank said he really kept his binoculars on the windowsill to watch me walking the beach in the morning without him to protect me from two-legged wolf sharks. I told him I didn't need a green flash to enjoy the flattery of being hot stuff or to see the truth in our hearts.

According to a Scottish Highland legend my father once told me, seeing the green flash sets you free of all illusions and falsehoods and you see clearly the truth in your own heart and the heart of your lover.

During the lingering winter of '92, Frank took his binoculars and drove to the Regina Airport several times to watch the sun go down. He said a guy with the nickname Eye would be able to see the fireball sun burst and refract a green flash of summer as it sunk into a white prairie sea.

Egyptians believed the brief emerald radiance was the "living light" of a supernatural message.

I have proof both beliefs are true.

This year I found a colour photograph Frank took after the sun had set and across the horizon there's a brilliant bluish-green streak. He never told me he saw the green flash through his camera lens. I can't tell if he took it through the hotel window at St. Pete's beach or the windshield of the car here in Regina. He might even have taken it across the lake from inside the cottage.

It doesn't matter.

Whenever I look at his photo, which is often since I can see it at night in the dark with my eyes closed, I feel Frank beside me, and hear him say, "I don't want to leave you, hon, but I'm not afraid to die."

Slipstream

In the slipstream of time between sleep and waking, I mix memory with desire, and Frank and I are in Sarasota. We're back in Florida's "*sarao sota – a place of dancing*," two Spanish words joined together as one.

I nudge Frank with my hip and hum overtures to "Amor" and "Besame Mucho," the two top songs of '43, the year we first locked eyes in high school. The bedroom windows of our rented condo at Castel del Mare are open and a soft salty breeze off the inland waterway carries April's sunrise flamenco music to us.

Storks clack-clatter in their platform nests of sticks on top of the tangled mangroves covering the mud islet bird sanctuary. Seagulls flying by to scavenge the beach at Siesta Key laugh in raucous yucca-yucca screeches. A swish of folding wings and a guttural croak announce the arrival of the snow-white heron in its sunny spot near our screened lanai, where it stands as still as a garden sculpture hoping to snatch a chameleon for breakfast. The pair of mourning doves nesting under the flowering oleander and azalea by our parking spot *kooo-krooo* in amorous harmony.

And so do we, the twosome of Saskatchewan snowbirds lying on the side of the twin bed next to the windows, listening.

When we get up, we'll put on the living room TV and turn to the local channel to hear the hotshot young news anchor we call Cronkite-light begin his weather riff by saying, "It's APDIP, Sunbirds, rise and shine." He'll promise blue skies dappled with cellophane clouds and heavenly high and low temperatures. Give the times of sunrise and sunset and high and low tide. Report ideal nautical conditions on the Gulf of Mexico. Do a variation of his opening theme that "Life's a beach on APDIP," and sign off saying, "That's the way it is." Frank will do a happy hip-hop, and say, "Let's beat our feet to a sand and surf treat, babe, it's APDIP again." The year-round residents and regular renters like us know that "APDIP" is the acronym of: *Another Perfect Day In Paradise*. And that *is* the way it is in April.

A sudden downdraft of clear air turbulence jolts me out of my reverie into cold reality. We're at home in Regina. Frank's cancer is back. I squeeze his hand. The malignant cells of non-Hodgkin's lymphoma have silently invaded his lymphatic system again. So much for got-it-all surgery and just-to-make-sure monthly chemo that kept us at home in April '92; the weekly chemo he began in May '93 after we got home from Sarasota, and undergoes now every weekday in '94. Third time lucky?

The lashing tail of the last March gale rattles the iced skeleton of the crabapple tree and whips a blizzard of sleet pellets at the glass of the closed bedroom window. Spring has sprung right over our province again. Here, in a place originally called Pile Of Bones, we're in the land of ten months of winter and two months of tough sledding.

Frank and I are wrapped together in our new down duvet on my side of the spooled walnut double bed I first slept in fifty-five years ago when I was nine years old. Here we are: two starry-eyed high school steadies nicknamed Eyeball and Butterball, Mr. and Mrs., Mom and Dad, Gran and Gramps, a couple of old huggers with our heads up above the covers.

Downstairs, asleep on his Snoopy pillow under his kitchen bench, a thirteen-year-old Terripoo named Scottie twitches as he dreams he's changed into a snarling Rottweiler named Fang to protect us from intruders.

Ten days ago, the day before cancerous cells showed up in Frank's checkup tests, when we brought our suitcases up from the basement to pack, Scottie sunk into his usual blue funk. He stretched out on the floor beside them with that hangdog look and wouldn't budge. Frank lifted Scottie's head off his paws, scratched him under the chin, and said, "Sorry, Fang, can't take you along to guard us in Florida. You might end up as a gator's hors d'oeuvre."

I shuddered. Last year, *The Sarasota Herald-Tribune* had a front-page story headlined: Large Gator Snatches Puppy As Stunned Owner Looks On. I clipped the article and it's probably in one of my Florida files. I don't want to remember that the puppy's name was Babe or that she was a six-week-old furry black spaniel with a white patch on her chest. Babe was on a leash leading her owner along a path around a lily pond when, without any warning, a rock became a swift-moving alligator that snatched and dragged the pup under the water. I can't forget that Babe yelped once and her owner said, "I heard her *weep*. Then she was gone."

Was the pup's fate a warning? At any rate, ever since Frank and I dismissed the pea-size lump behind his left ear as a swollen gland, we've taken special notice of the warning signs that danger lurks in paradise.

Our rented car no longer had Air Flite bumper stickers nor a license plate that identified it as a rental. And above the polite "Seat Belts Fastened?" on the dash, a block-lettered sign stated: Locked Doors Stop Carjackers.

The condo had a smiley face sticker on the kitchen window with the emergency phone number of the company providing twenty-four-hour security patrols.

A flyer directed at residents of the older open-gated complexes built in the late 1970s or early 1980s such as ours at Castel del Mare advised us to: Lock Windows And Doors And Buy A New Armedguard Air Conditioner To Protect Loved Ones And Possessions From Home Invasions.

Preventing the outward signs of ageing was a hot topic in the retirement paradise of the universe where consumers only had to reach age fifty to be entitled to a senior discount. How to look too young to pay less and need to show your ID was the message of ads in tabloids and magazines displayed in supermarkets open 24/7 and on TV. They promised that a decade or more would vanish from sight after a facelift, breast implants or propping up, penile enhancement, hair removal or grafts, teeth capping, lip plumping, tummy tucks, fat suction, nose bobbing, or buying an entirely new identity with the complete body makeover sex change. Looking older than one did ten or twenty years ago was something to avoid at all costs. Any thought of death should be dealt with by closure. Laughing on the outside without laugh lines was to be desired, crying on the inside, not. Surgery was the passport to Shangri-la.

Our old friends at home seemed to look the same as they had in high school without cosmetic surgery. Their sags, bags, and wrinkles were only transparent masks over their young faces. In Florida we'd gotten to know a few people a little bit since the early '70s when we started renting at Castel del Mare. Frank and I were in our forties then, and the few newly retired couples we became friendly with were fifteen or more years older than us. We hadn't seen any of them for a year and eleven months when we went back last year.

Ruth and Rusty lived next door to the first condo we'd rented for seven years. They'd retired to Sarasota from the northern USA in 1967 and were the original owners of their condo. Ruth worked part-time at home, printing books for the blind on her braillewriter. She had CPD (chronic pulmonary disease) and strapped on a portable oxygen tank when she went down to the terrace by the round pool on weekday afternoons to play mahjong. Rusty was a retired major league baseball umpire. It was a second marriage for both of them and obviously a happy one. Ruth said the only major adjustment she'd made was to go outside the house where the neighbours could see her while Rusty was watching a baseball game on television. If she stayed inside and watched with him, she said anyone within shouting distance would think that Rusty's swearing and yelling were directed at her. The last time Frank and I saw Rusty he was slowly recovering from throat cancer and living dangerously by swimming in the oblong family pool early every morning doing dog-paddle laps with his neck stretched up and his head tipped back so the water didn't get in his tracheotomy. Rusty died in the Presbyterian Pines Hospice in 1992 and Ruth was confined to her second-floor condo on oxygen full time. She'd sold their condo and arranged to move to the Pines before Easter. I went up to see her as soon as I heard.

Her door was open and she was sitting in a swivel chair in front of the open sliding door to the big balcony that overlooked the inland waterway. Except for the large oxygen tank she was hooked to, she looked as perky and sporty as a *Vogue* ad for gaining eternal youth naturally.

"It's APDIP again," she greeted me, and we laughed.

Ruth was the one who had told Frank and me what APDIP meant. I said Frank and I were really sad to learn Rusty had died a year ago.

"He was like a fish out of water when he got too weak to swim. He went to the Pines to die," she said. She swivelled her chair around, held up her hands, and dancing her fingers at the view down the waterway, said in a soft breathless voice, "I'll have the dots and points of this paradise printed on my soul wherever I go."

Ruth's hobby was painting and she was a talented artist, I think. I looked at her painting of the lion with its flowing mane almost the same colour as Rusty's hair used to be and the tawny lioness lying beside him at the edge of the vivid green jungle. Her large oil painting was the only picture left hanging on the wall. Across the nearly empty living room from the majestic lion and lioness there was a tall white rattan unit that had a few plates and ornaments on its shelves. Ruth told me to choose something from it to take home to Canada. I picked a small seashell pelican. Ruth breathed deeply through the oxygen tubes in her nostrils, and said: "A wonderful bird is the pelican / His bill will hold more than his belican / He can take in his beak / Food enough for a week / But I'm darned if I see how the helican."

She took another long deep breath, and continued at high speed: "Dickson L. Merritt wrote that verse, not Ogden Nash as most people think. Rusty made the pelican when we first retired down here. He'll be dancing a Scottish reel that you want it. Do you know what the shells are?"

I said, "No."

"Hand it to me," she said, and closed her eyes after I did. She held it in the palm of her right hand and ran the fingertips of her left hand over it. "This little white pelican is two inches in height and has a Scotch Bonnet head, a Welk face and bill, Scallop body, and its radial ribbed feet are Cockleshells you touch for luck in love."

Rusty's pelican sits on our mantle on top of a ceramic jar embossed with pink pelicans done by the well-known Canadian pottery artist Victor Cicansky. I'd planned to visit Ruth at the Pines while we were in Sarasota this April and take her a photo of it in its place of honour in our living room. But we would have arrived three months too late. I found that out last week when I phoned the condominium office and one of the other mah-jong players answered. She said Ruth had decided to have her oxygen stopped on New Year's Eve morning and she'd slipped away quietly that night to welcome 1994 with Rusty.

The biggest shock I had last year was finding out what Per had done. Having a wash-and-wear haircut and perm at Per's International Hair in the small but trendy Boatyard Mall next door to the condo was a tradition I established when the shop opened in the Eighties. I had a standing appointment with Per for the first Monday in April and had dropped in to confirm it because I hadn't been able to keep it in '92. The salon's slogan was: *Per hair has flair*. When the woman at the reception desk said Per was no longer with them, I asked if he'd decided to stay in Norway after his summer holidays there. The three women hairdressers stopped cutting, curling and combing and stared at me. It took quite a while before the sad story came out.

Despondent over a nasty breakup with his long-time girl-friend, Per had gone to KMart, bought a gun and ammunition, and shot himself in the powder room behind the reception desk. Everybody began to talk at once. Pointing scissors, tongs, brush and a hairdryer at the closed door and cutting each other off in staccato phrases, they said: "On the last Saturday in March; noon on the 27th; walked through the shop full of customers with the rifle hidden under his jacket; locked the door; nobody could get in and stop him; beyond help; a crackling blast like a lightning bolt; everybody screaming; blood and stuff everywhere."

Silence.

"Per kept a card on each of his clients," the receptionist said. "Do you want to see yours?"

I said, "Well, okay, I guess so."

On my card, Per had written: *Nice woman. Has a good sense of humour. Likes a laugh. Easy care hair.*

Oh, God, I thought, all I can think of to say is Per almost laughed out loud when we first met and I said all I knew about Scandinavians was the taunt: Three Swedes ran through the weeds chased by one Norwegian.

As Easter and Passover and spring break approached, dire warnings about Florida wildlife were featured in the local Sarasota media.

We were surprised to see on TV that what we'd thought were clusters of big sea oak leaves floating in the shallows of the Gulf were actually venomous stingrays. I tucked my feet underneath me on the chair as we watched one drive its sawtooth tail spine into a wooden boat.

An article about people being terrorized by wild Muscovy ducks caused us to stop parking under our shade tree near their nesting place at Crescent Beach. The greenish-black and white ducks with red faces looked so comically sedate waddling about like overfed gentlemen at their club. But apparently when they chased someone, shaking the enflamed red carbuncles around their eyes and bills, nipping at heels and lunging up for bites of flesh, they were prehistoric winged carnivores.

Gators made frequent appearances in the newspaper. The headlines were lighthearted. For the one snoozing in front of a mall entrance door, it was: Shopped Till He Dropped Gator Awaits Mate. The photo of an alert gator outside the locked gate of a caged swimming pool, watching the family inside, was captioned: Gator Eyes Caged Meat.

A wordless warning to be prepared for danger was portrayed by the only picture on the otherwise bare walls of our condo. I identified with the life-sized kink-necked egret standing in a lily pond with its head twisted round over its back and one leg tucked up ready for flight. The large print was hung high over the chesterfield, only about eight inches from the ceiling, and was so crooked it was almost sideways. A belated April fool's joke, we decided, someone's idea of whistling past the graveyard. Getting up there to straighten it without a ladder would definitely be dangerous, we agreed, although we both had the urge to do it. The tipsy egret was a focal point that made us laugh.

I stood on the chesterfield, posed like the egret, and Frank took my photo. Then I took his. Frank set the camera's timer and we posed together, holding hands.

The mayday punch line to the joke happened after we got home. Frank took our films to Safeway to be developed and the entire egret roll was blank. He announced it in a charade of the egret's stance, shook his head from side to side, flapped his arms, stared at me with the white of his eyes until I said, "The bird flew the coop."

We didn't need snapshots to remember the condo's decor. Unlike the show home condition of the three other two-bed/two-bath units we'd rented in a dozen years of going to Castel Del Mare, the egret surveyed sunbelt decay. I listed the 1993 condo's cons and pros on my laptop computer.

NEGATIVES:

– *This condo has sixties wall-to-wall, musty smelling and matted, gold shag carpet. Who knows what evil creepy-crawly critters live and die in it?*

– *The kitchen floor is the original lino and many of its dark olive green tiles have curled up corners to stub a toe on or trip over.*

– *The kitchen countertop has obviously been used as a cutting board.*

– *No microwave oven.*

– *Some of the smoky grey mirror tiles covered with gold scribbles glued on the dining area wall have fallen off and are stuck together in a stack on the floor.*

POSITIVES:

– *Has an excellent radio but we can't find Public Radio on it.*

– *The condo's location near Avenue D on the ground floor. It's sort of homey to back on private houses and see the man in the bungalow behind us work in the yard and the woman hang their laundry.*

– *The pair of raccoons that stroll by the lanai every evening and make us miss Scottie barking.*

– *A stately white heron that waits in the sun by the screened lanai to catch chameleons and to be fed sardines by us.*

Sarasota 1994? Cancelled for this year. We'd signed the contract and paid the final, non-refundable portion of the rent on a condo that was a dream. It had been completely renovated, tastefully decorated, had new furniture and appliances, plus excellent lighting beside each comfortable place to read, including on both sides of the queen-size bed in the master bedroom. The only good thing about the late cancellation we had to make was that the condo owners refunded all the rent we'd paid without any penalty and wrote us to say they hoped Frank's cancer treatments were one hundred percent successful and we'd be able to rent their place for April 1995.

So did we. Passionately.

We recall their place as being lemon fresh. The dingy interior of our '93 condo smelled like a mouldy orange. But we weren't inside much in the daytime. We walked the beach, swam in the pool, ate out at early bird specials, went to movie matinees, took afternoon car trips to explore the Gulf coast, and went shopping – Frank reluctantly.

Sarasota Square Mall's expansion to double its former huge size made it a formidable place to shop. Uniformed guards with their hands on holstered guns turned their heads like robots looking for a human target. I wanted to dive for cover at every loud noise. I distracted myself by concentrating on finding the world's greatest bargain. I succeeded the day Frank and I agreed to split and meet in two hours at the circle of benches under the skylight at the JCPenney inside entrance.

I was a bit late and I hadn't found a bargain. I went to the centre of the circle and turned slowly, searching the waiting men. Frank wasn't one of them. Or was he? He always arrived and departed on time. I circled the circle, inside and out. In

Regina, I can do a quick scan of a crowd for white hair and find him. Not in Florida. I broke the rule we made travelling in Europe with the kids to never leave the planned meeting place. Finally found a male clerk in JCPenney's Sporting Goods to look for Frank in the men's washroom and dressing rooms at men's wear. Left the Mall to see if he was in the car, dozing or reading. Went back and looked round and round the circle until I was dizzy. Had he been kidnapped? Mugged? Murdered? Then, turning my head like a robot and praying he was okay so I could kill him, I began walking toward the centre of the mall.

I nearly dropped dead when he took my arm, and said, "Hey, good lookin', want to pick up a bargain? Here I am."

Thank God, I thought, and glared at him.

He said, "I was on time. But the benches were full of guys. I stood there and waited thirty-two minutes before I went over to Lerner's Spring Break display where I've been lying on the lounge under the beach umbrella for twenty-one minutes. Lots of pretty women asked if I was on sale. One young gal ran her fingers through my hair as she passed and told her boyfriend it sure felt real for a mannequin."

I snorted.

On the way back to the condo, Frank kept saying, "You were late." And I kept replying, "You were hiding."

About 300 feet from our left turn at Avenue D, we were held up in the traffic waiting for the Stickney Point Road drawbridge to go down. I stared out my window on the passenger side. The three well-dressed black men were standing near the table in the screened porch of the newly renovated mobile home. They were in the porch somewhere every time we drove by. Their constant presence was what made us realize how few black people we ever

saw working in the stores or restaurants or at the tourist attrac-
tions we went to, such as Selby Gardens or Mote Marine
Museum. Once, walking the beach, we'd seen two little black
girls in a daycare group of white children, but they were the only
other black people we'd seen in the area. We were curious about
what the black men were doing, why they never sat down. Did
they live there? Were they visiting? I rolled down the window to
take a closer look.

"The air conditioning's on," Frank said.

I said, "Hey, those black guys are cardboard!" Sentinels? Store
displays?

"Happens," Frank said, "waiting for shopoholic women..."
and he sang, "...who want to buy a paper doll that they can call
their own."

"Found the same old bargain today I latched onto long ago
and far away." I rolled up the window. "I was late."

"I hid," he said. "So the deal's still on."

We hooked our little fingers together and in unison, said,
"Divorce never; murder maybe."

It's strange, but these wintry spring days at home have a safe
inside-out feeling to them that helps relieve the tension of
why we couldn't fly south.

We make do with talk, watch TV in the evening with our eyes
closed, have family and friends drop in to visit, celebrate
anniversaries known only to us, remember funny things the kids
did, and read each other's thoughts – not all of them happy.

Codes

hy doesn't a good attitude cure cancer?

Frank accentuates the positive about his treatments. He calls them, "My infusions of deadly chemicals to kill every seed of cancer, but not quite me." If I fuss too much about how he's feeling, he croons, "You've got to latch on to the affirmative, hon, and don't mess with misery in between."

Every weekday morning, when I drive Frank to the clinic to have three hours of chemo, we play a good luck game our nine-year-old granddaughter Alexis taught us. The first one to see the jellybean-red Volkswagen parked on Twenty-Fifth Avenue pokes the other one, and says, "Red punch buggy, no return." It will be a win-win situation for both the poker and the poked when our hope comes true that the new chemo brew kills cancer. On the way to the clinic yesterday morning, Frank saw the bug first. It's always gone by the time I've picked Frank up and we're driving home, but it was still sitting there yesterday covered with a tarp, and we did a duet.

"Snug as a bug in a rug," we said in unison, poking each other. Then we did a double high-five, Alexis' style, for twice the luck to cover today's chemo holiday.

Today is Good Friday and the cancer clinic is closed. And, according to a "This Day In History" item on the radio this morning, in an occurrence so rare that 1994 is only the fourth and the last year it happens in the twentieth century, Good Friday is also April Fool's Day. Before Pope Gregory created the new Gregorian calendar that was adopted in the 1500s, April 1 was New Year's Day. Those who forgot that the date had been changed to January 1 and kept celebrating became known as April fools. The item ended with an instrumental chorus of "Auld Lang Syne" and a voice-over warning to watch out for salt in the sugar bowl.

"Love is the salt of life," Frank said, and we had a clinch and kiss to welcome a solemn religious day and a silly secular one meant for fun.

We're at home, doing our own thing, when I hear the old song I've fallen in love with all over again.

"I Can See Clearly Now" beams its sunny tune from the kitchen TV as I leave the laundry room.

"Ad's on, hon," Frank calls, and turns up the volume.

I'm already standing behind him, a stack of warm folded towels in my arms, smiling at the picture. Ears perked, tails swinging, a dog and pup tilt their heads from side to side as they watch a big sunflower on a TV screen sway to the tune like an exotic tropical metronome. They're descendants of the RCA fox terrier whose head is cocked at the gramophone horn listening to his master's voice.

I look down at Scottie, curled into a fuzzy ball asleep on the breakfast nook bench beside his master. Dogs he can't sniff don't interest him.

The music ends too fast and Frank zaps the yap-yap of that damn no-medical-questions-asked ad for life insurance.

"Know what I want to do?" I ask.

"Adopt a puppy from the animal shelter to keep Scottie company while I'm hooked up at the clinic," Frank says. "And buy a record of your sunshiny day song at Vintage Vinyl so we can listen to more than twelve seconds of it, I'll bet."

"Mind reader," I say. "Poor pooch is so sulky when I come home without you, he just lies with his nose pressed against the crack under the door, waiting. He won't even look up at me when I tell him he's a good boy for taking care of the house and offer him his c-o-o-k-i-e."

Scottie lifts his head. Frank pats it, and says, "You know what she spelled, don't you, old boy?"

Sunshiny days. I keep hoping we still have years and years of them to look forward to. I can see all the obstacles in our way by looking over Frank's shoulder at the array of pill bottles on the table and the medication chart he's updating on graph paper. Codes for everything: Nyaderm (NY); Nu-Ranitidine (RAG); Prednisone (P) – crossed out and replaced with (SKYROID), the nickname Alexis gave his high-flying steroid; Apo-Allopurinol (AP); Nu-Cotrimox-DS (NX); even Swish & Swallow (SS) and his mouthwash (MW). The times to take them are listed according to the twenty-four hour clock. It looks like an airline schedule.

Frank walks his fingers across the top of his sky blue ball cap with *Siesta Key, Fla.* on it and airy mesh vents at the sides. It's the one he always wears the first morning we walk the beach after our arrival in Sarasota.

He claims he wears his caps backwards for three good reasons: baseball players believe it's good luck; Alexis says he looks cool; and, without a visor, he knows that a direct gaze of his brown eyes into my blue eyes melts me.

He turns and says, "Guess I'm pulling a bad April fool joke to wear this one today when we're grounded in Regina."

"Scottie's not complaining we're at home instead of on Crescent Beach without him," I say. I look up at the poster I bought last April that almost covers the wall under the kitchen clock. "Why don't we take our ferocious guard dog on our first kitchen beach w-a-l-k?"

Scottie leaps off the bench, skids to the back door, tugs his harness and leash off the peg, and prances back dragging them behind him. Frank fastens the harness around him, attaches the leash, gives Scottie a boost back up on the bench, tells him to stay, takes a deep breath, and says, "Nice whiff of fish in that salty air, eh Scott?"

I put the bath towels down on his chart and sit on the bench beside Scottie. "And icing sugar sand that's springy as perogy dough at the shore where it's damp."

We sit silently for a minute, lined up on the bench like pelicans on the rail of the Sunshine Skyway, all three of us looking straight ahead at the whimsical poster of Siesta Key. Hibiscus and oleander blossoms and palm fronds frame a map of fun-in-the-sun activities: college kids play volleyball; a family sculpts a sand manatee; hotshots on Jet Skis buzz the beach; a boy standing on a beach board skims along the last lap of waves unfolding on the shore; dolphins arc over the brilliant blue water in the midst of swimmers and sailboats; and a woman beneath a rainbow-striped parachute linked to a red speedboat floats high in the sapphire sky over the Gulf. The only walker on the poster's beach is a barefoot pot-bellied man wearing cut-off jeans, his grey hair in a long ponytail and his gnarled legs comically drawn like wide open scissors.

"Only guys walking the beach will be that hairy old hippy and me, a geriatric Big C skinhead," Frank mutters.

"Hey, bald is in. It's sexy," I say. "Lucky you've got such a nicely shaped head, no scars, dents or bumps."

Frank lifts his cap, takes my hand and guides it slowly around his bare head, much to poor Scottie's consternation at being passed over.

"Yep, round and smooth and hard as a billiard ball. Not even a small bump of knowledge," I tell him.

I can feel the band-aids on his inner wrist. He has a patchwork of them up both arms on his punctured veins. Next week he's having a stainless steel *Hickman* port implanted in his chest for the chemo needles.

He puts his cap back on frontward. "Got to shade my eyes from the sun." He looks at his digital watch. "Think we can do the two miles to Point of Rocks, touch the stone wall for good luck, and be back in an hour for our swim and rejuvenation rest?"

"Give me a hand jumping the stream of sulphurous water in the storm channel, and let's take off," I say. We grin at each other.

"Hey, hey, hey, there goes that other pair of hand holders, burning up the beach," Frank says. "Got new matching Spandex bathing suits, I see."

"And she hasn't gained an ounce." I splay my hand from my left boob to my belly roll. Does the roll stick out farthest? Getting Frank's weight up cooking his favourite meals is fattening. He's lost thirteen pounds and I've found them. I straighten my back and focus on who else it will be fun to see again walking the beach.

"Tarzan, drool-drool. No Jane in sight yet, but I can spot his sleek physique a mile away. Is he a primal scream hunk, or what?" I do a subdued rendition of a coyote howl I perfected in high school as a reply to two-legged wolves.

Scottie's ears fly up and he growls like a purring cat.

"Hah! Wear your prescription sunglasses tomorrow and get a good look," Frank says. "Six-feet tall, but he's sure as hell not young. Has his hairy old nose stuck up in the air so he can't smell his rancid sun oil."

I laugh. We have this dispute every year. Tarzan and Jane are both tall, six feet plus, somewhere in their upper seventies, I'd say. And, although Jane's a little more stooped over each year, she stays as boyishly slim as a couturier's model. True, Tarzan's stuck-up. He never slows his animal amble to look down on us and reply to our "Good morning," or to let Jane catch up to him. Yes, he's a bit full of himself, but damn good to look at. He always has a ripe walnut tan and his belly's as flat as the movie Tarzan's was back in the early forties.

Ah, there's the rub. No pot. Frank's stomach used to be a steel plate. When we were in high school, he knocked the bobby socks off girls by imitating King Kong to show off the strength of his solar plexus. He pounded his chest doing teeth-bared snarls and growled at onlookers to hit him in the gut as hard as they could with their heads, fists, or World Progress history texts. I used to shut my eyes and plug my ears.

If I do that now, I see my father at the dining room table looking at breast tumour slides. I hear him call me in, and say, "See this dark mass? Trauma to undeveloped glandular tissue could have caused that cancer." My father died in 1948 when I was eighteen so I never got to talk to him as an adult. I wish I could ask him now if blows to Frank's stomach could have caused his lymphatic cancer.

Frank nudges me. "To your left, quick, Mick and Min are scurrying out of the archway at Crescent Arms, ignoring each other, as usual."

Mick and Min have tiny sun-browned bodies. Trim. Neat. Muscles toned. Their mouse ears are black headphones. Side by side, listening to little transistor radios strapped around their waists instead of to the surf or seagulls or each other, in quick tiny steps, they march down the beach like a pair of militant mice.

"And here's Bronze Boy, Gillette's ad for a sexy head babes love to kiss." Frank tilts his head toward mine. Scottie gives Frank's ear a lick and flops down to nap.

Bronze Boy's bald-pate is a lustrous metallic brown. It glistens in the sun as he strolls up and down the beach showing off his Atlas physique. I'm glad Frank saw him and made fun of my earlier gaffe.

The hardest things for me to resist are taking over his illness as mine or being a Pollyanna about every setback. Like, bald is "sexy?" To a guy who watched his mane of white hair stream down his body and plug the drain of the shower? "Better bald than dead," he said as he cleaned the drain. "It'll grow back."

"Whoa," I say, "there's Wild Bill Necklock, the bowlegged wrestler who eats his straw hat for extra fibre."

"He'll be choking down Questran to plug himself up if he eats that black sombrero haystack," Frank says.

Code (Q), the chalky powder Frank took to prevent diarrhea, is no longer on his chart. I didn't see what his codes are for the laxative and stool softener he needs now to counteract the constipating effects of codeine.

"Good to see Lady Hip-out-of-joint escaped her soggy daffodil garden in England again to soak up some Sarasota sun." Frank tips his cap.

Daffodils – April – cancer month – I run my hand lightly down Frank's arm, then along the curve of dozing Scottie's spine. "Our watchdog's enjoying his own make-believe and name game," Frank says. "He's twitching to snap awake as Fang."

Non-Hodgkin's lymphoma and chemotherapy at the cancer clinic named in memory of my father aren't make-believe or a name game. For years, my father's name was the only one used when Frank was introduced as the chap who married his eldest daughter, leaving us both nameless. Seeing my father's name everywhere at the clinic makes me angry with him for letting himself die of a heart attack before he found a cure for cancer.

Frank taps the tops of a row of pill bottles, then looks up at the poster, shakes his head, and says, "Sun, sand and surf sure beat what's on my plate as fix-me-ups."

I decide not to see Ghost Writer drifting along the beach. Visualizing a hooded spectre wrapped in a long white terry cloth shroud, face lathered with white sunscreen, might remind Frank his immune system is shot to smithereens. Alexis made signs on her computer for our doors that say: WARNING - IF YOU HAVE A COLD OR THE FLU, PLEASE DO NOT VISIT IN PERSON, PHONE.

"Hey," Frank says, "isn't that Miss Crick-in-the-neck collecting shells? Looks lonely as ever, eh?"

"That's her," I say, and think how lonely I would be if seashells were all that whispered in my ear.

Frank looks at his watch. "Better not stop to see Ms. Blackbelt in her black kimono doing combat. Let's touch our lucky stone in the wall and head back."

"Oh, come on," I say. "Let's see if she has any new moves to use against her invisible opponent."

I admire the way she leaps into fighting position, elbows up, arms open, ready to grab and fling that covert attacker over her shoulder. She freezes, kicks – first with one leg, then the other – turns slightly as she leaps again, freezes, straight-arms the air, and repeats her routine until her unseen enemy is defeated.

"Wonder what our friends call us? Nudge-nudge, wink-wink," Frank says, the cue for our corny routine at the end of our first beach walk. It doesn't sound as if Frank's heart is in it.

I look at him out of the corner of my eye. It always shocks me how clearly a sideways glance lets me see what he really looks like. His teeth are too big when he smiles and his Prednisone-puffed cheeks are the colour of skim milk.

To answer Frank's question, I think the other beach walkers call us Tum and Bum. Last summer, when my mother was ready to take our photo on our forty-third wedding anniversary and I whispered to Frank to suck in his gut, Mother said, "He'll tuck in his tummy if you hold in your rear end, dear." I follow our script.

"Is your face red from trying to tuck in your tummy while that rare pair of young chicks in bikinis you didn't see passed us, or because you were planning a seduction as soon as we're back at the condo?"

He tries to smile, then winks as he turns his cap backwards, and says, "Guess it's pretty obvious why they call us Loverboy and Sexpot, eh?" But his voice lacks conviction.

We turn toward each other and come together in an awkward old pals' clinch, wrapping our arms around each other, almost squashing Scottie. He yips excitedly as he tries to struggle up between us and slobber us with kisses.

I blow in Frank's ear, and whisper, "I'm going upstairs, Loverboy." I stand up, look at the stack of towels on his medication chart, pause, and we glance at each other. The master bathroom vanity of last year's condo had a card on it with a cupid in the upper left corner aiming an arrow at the message:

LOVE is...
leaving the towels behind
Thank you!

"Don't even think about leaving them there, thank you," he says. "I have to memorize my codes for the new stuff I'm on. Love is leaving me to get on with it."

That's what I do. I pick up the cold towels and head upstairs to put them away.

There's a trick I'm learning to do. I step aside and watch us as if we're in a cancer-can-be-beaten ad on TV. Sometimes, like I do now, I switch channels to a rerun of when we were young and smitten with lust.

One shiny night in April 1950, I helped Frank do his homework for his new airline career. I see us clearly.

He's my guy and I'm his gal. We're sitting at the kitchen table at my house. My family is out. I cooked for him to show off my housewifery skills, which were nil.

The cupcakes I made from the recipe in my mother's wartime *Victory Cook Book*, compiled by the Knox United Church Friendship Circle, turned out to be as hard as the India rubber ball I played "Easy Ivy Over" with as a girl.

That was a shock. The Circle members were all devout believers that the way to a man's heart is through his stomach.

My mother said every one of their usually secret recipes proved they were right. And the lyrics of one of my father's favourite songs asked Billy Boy: *Can she bake a cherry pie/quick as a man can wink his eye?*

So what went wrong? Sabotage? Had I misread the damn code?

CHOCOLATE FLUFFS
1 tbsp. butter
1½ squares Bakers chocolate
Melt together and add
1 tsp. vanilla
1 tsp. soda (put in sour milk)
¼ tsp. salt
⅔ cup white sugar
1 cup sour milk (add tbsp. vinegar to fresh milk)
1½ cups of cake flour
Bake 15 minutes at 350

I thought the eggs had been left out by mistake and added some. And I didn't have a clue that all purpose flour wasn't the same as cake flour. Still, after ruining a few, I was able to follow the instructions and carve the top off one of the batch, dig a pit in the centre, fill it with whipped cream, and set the little dunce hat back on.

"This is too delicious to eat fast," Frank keeps saying when he isn't chewing, and then asks if there's any whipped cream left in the bowl.

I watch him eating his heart out for me. His brush cut makes his thick curly hair look like woven wicker.

My hair is as black as the one he finds in his last helping of whipped cream and discreetly tucks in the vest pocket of his jacket – over his heart.

Oh, he looks so handsome. He's wearing his new navy blue gabardine Trans-Canada Airlines uniform. It finally arrived ten weeks after he was hired as a passenger agent. The dress code requires him to wear a white shirt, a TCA navy and dark red striped necktie, navy or black executive socks, and black oxfords. That's how he's dressed, except for the socks. He has on the multicoloured argyle socks I knit him for his twenty-third birthday on February 23rd. The pattern was really complicated; counting stitches and switching from one colour of wool to another – red, blue, yellow, green – was confusing. Untangling wool takes time. Casting-off was a problem. One sock is a tourniquet that barely covers his calf. The other one would cover his knee if it would stay up, but it's as wide as a windsock.

Diamond socks, diamond ring glittering on my finger. Sometimes a diamond chip that flashes one point of light is brighter than a karat flashing many.

I use my left hand to go down the International Civil Aviation Authority list of three-letter codes for airports as I quiz Frank on them – the easiest one first.

"YQR?" I ask.

"Regina," we both answer. Even I know home base.

Then it gets tougher. I fire the codes, he shoots back answers: YQV? Yorkton. YWG? Winnipeg. YBR? Brandon. YOW? Ottawa, tax town. YUL? Montreal, Head Office...and on, and on, until I can say, "Perfect touchdown on the tarmac of every TCA destination – in YZ?"

"Canada," he answers.

Time out for congratulation kisses.

Then, ring finger raised, I move my hand down a list of air-line lingo: Con? Contingency pass-holder travelling on a seat-available basis. Bumped? What happens to a Con if paying passengers buy all the seats. Fam-flight? Familiarization flight for a new employee and spouse.

More kisses. The future is shinier than my diamond. It glows brighter than the gold wedding band I'm wearing six months later when we take our fam-flight on the evening milk run to Winnipeg.

Neither one of us has ever been up in an airplane before, but my husband is an expert on procedures.

When we're seated, Frank illustrates the two takeoffs and landings we'll have on the way there and returning the next day. Gliding his hand up and down, he says, "YQR to YQV to YWG. We'll have a room service dinner and a good night's sleep in luxury. Leave YWG, fly to YBR, land, take off again up into blue skies, touch down at YQR, and we're home on the range in the Queen City of the plains."

"Once we're airborne, it'll be just like sitting in our own living room for four hours," Frank says as we taxi out to the end of the runway.

He takes my hand in his as the DC-3 Skyliner accelerates from a rough purr to a shuddering roar.

When the engines grind down to a grumbling growl, he lets go of my damp hand, strokes my ring finger, and says, "See? Smooth as sil –"

And the sudden thunderous jackhammer thrust of the real takeoff, not the full-throttle instrument check at the end of the runway, plasters us against the back of our seats, faces white as sheets.

There's a similarity of my feelings then and now.

Gliding down through the sunshine on our fourth and final descent into Regina, Frank pats the DC-3's fuselage, and says, "Thanks to this workhorse, and our second honeymoon night in the Fort Garry Hotel, we're getting to be old hands at the rhythm of ups and downs."

He expects me to laugh sexily, and I do.

Even now, while I'm putting towels away and Frank's coding pills, I think, what a wonderful flight we're on.

Down in the Valley

The glacier shaped the sunken garden of Qu'Appelle Valley in Saskatchewan's prairie and the meltwater river spreads out along its meandering course in lakes like ours. Mythic, magic, and, yes, spiritual, Lake Katepwa began to call us down in the valley to our family gathering place on July 1st before the Ice Age.

Or, as Mother says, "From before ice cubes existed for my G and T." Her mother, my favourite grandmother, Sophie (Fisher) Wilson, set the matriarchal pattern of moving to the lake with the children for July and August. She began taking her first three children and a milk cow to camp at Katepwa in 1902 when my mother Florence was just five months old.

I was four months old in May 1930 when my parents first brought me from my Alabama birthplace to the lake in the 1929 Model A roadster Grandpa Wilson bought them. My father liked to wisecrack that I could swim like a fish because I'd gone from Montreal to the Detroit Ford factory and on to Tuscaloosa swimming in Mother's womb.

"And flutter kicking like a whale," Mother added. "On your

return trip to Canada you were a sweet Southern belle sitting in your canvas car chair gurgling *Da-Da.*"

While teaching at the University School of Medicine, my father spent most of his summer breaks in three-month residencies learning to diagnose and treat cancer. In 1933, he decided to drive to his late May residency at Johns Hopkins Hospital in Baltimore first and to Katepwa afterwards. He drove Mother and me, my year-old brother Kenny and our black nurse-maid Lily Owens to Chicago in our new family-size Ford and we took the train to Indian Head.

Before we moved down to Granny's cottage at Katepwa, Lily and I walked downtown every day to get the mail. As we passed Nichols Bros. Gas & Service the first day, Al Nichols called to his brothers, "Here's A.E. and Sophie Wilson's Yankee grand-gal."

I stopped, stamped my foot, and said, "I'm not a damn Yankee. I'm a Southerner!"

He laughed, then took Lily and me to the Rainbow Café for ice cream cones. After that, it was almost a daily occurrence for one of the Nichols brothers or a customer to greet me as a Yankee so I'd do my ice cream routine.

But my role as a summer visitant to Saskatchewan from the Deep South was soon passé. The next year, in May 1934, we crossed the border into Canada and stayed. Instead of going home to Tuscaloosa from Katepwa in 1934, we went to Winnipeg where my father was Senior Resident in Surgery at the General Hospital.

From August 1935 to August 1936, he studied at New York Memorial Hospital for Cancer and Allied Diseases and, as Mother boasted, after six months he was the first Canadian ever to be awarded a Rockefeller Fellowship. Mother and Kenny and

I stayed in Indian Head and I started school. Our rented house was across the Unknown Soldier Park from the railroad station and the midnight through-train disturbed my sleep. One night I dreamt I was crossing the University of Alabama quad with my father to see his black widow spiders and lost hold of his hand when the hornets rumbled out of Denny Chimes Tower and stung me until I screamed myself awake.

In 1936-37, my father took my mother with him on a freighter to Great Britain when he went to do a nine-month survey of cancer treatment centres there and in France, Belgium, Germany and Sweden. Gran Sophie looked after Kenny in Indian Head. I stayed in Regina with Uncle Wilf, Aunt Lola and cousin Gordon, who was in my grade at Lakeview School.

My parents were moving around so much it sometimes seemed that the cottage at Katepwa was our only real home. But after they came back from overseas, my father got his first job as a cancer specialist and we moved to Toronto. He'd been a radiologist at Toronto General Hospital for nearly two years when he came home one day and asked Kenny and me how we'd like to live in Regina.

"My hometown," he said, and winked at Mother.

"An hour's drive from Katepwa," she said.

"Well," I said. "I've already lived there, but..."

Mother said, "Your father's time at the lake won't be just a few weekends when we arrive and some dog days of August before a five-day road trip to Tuscaloosa or Toronto."

We arrived in May 1939 and our resident doctor got in the swing of things to do at the lake right away. His prescriptions included: shed shoes immediately on arrival so bare feet receive the earth's electricity; celebrate the past, present and future on the Eve of July 1st round a bonfire singing songs, storytelling, then a midnight swim.

The eve of Dominion Day 1941 and the story he told keeps replaying in my thoughts lately like a 3D movie titled CLAWS.

M y father is pleased as punch with the spectacular log pyramid he built for a bonfire to welcome the start of our summer holidays July 1st. Everybody is ready and waiting for it to be lit.

The dirty thirties lowered the lake level and left plenty of room for all of us on the shore: my kid brother Kenny and eleven-month-old baby sister Heather on Mother's lap; a choir of aunts and uncles; and a crowd of cousins.

Helen and I are the oldest cousins. She's fourteen and I'm eleven. We act blasé about what's next.

The lighting ceremony, two days after my parents' wedding anniversary on June 28, is always a bit mushy. Mother is sitting on the Spooning Stone. My father goes over, puts his hand under her chin to raise her face up closer to his, and asks, "What's the shape of a kiss?" Before she can answer, he says, "Give me one and I'll call it square," then kisses her. The boy cousins boo. Helen and I shrug. He kisses Heather's forehead, Mother's lips again and then, with a magician's flourish, strikes a wooden match on the seat of his pants and lights the bonfire in five places before the match burns out.

As the flames lick the sky, we all stand at attention and sing "O Canada." It's wartime and the Nazis invaded Russia without warning before school was out in June. My father is a surgeon lieutenant in the Naval Reserve and does physicals at HMCS

Queen in the Regina Winter Club beside Wascana Creek. He orders us to sing "O Canada" loud enough to be heard by our boys overseas. When we sing, "Stand on guard for thee..." Helen and I turn our heads for a furtive glance at the lake. There aren't any ominous shadowy blotches on the water – not yet.

Before long, as my father scientifically designed it to do, the pyramid of bone-dry poplar tree trunks collapses into the square firepit bordered by rocks. After we burn our mouths on black marshmallows, we sing the sad songs round the embers; "My Bonnie Lies Over The Ocean," "Down In The Valley," "Clementine" – who falls into the foaming brine, and is lost and gone forever – until it's time for the sleepy little cousins to be carried up the path to bed. Then, to the tune of "Round And Round The Mulberry Bush," we sing seven rounds of the lake lullaby: "Seven men slept in a sleeping porch bed / roll over, roll over / they all rolled over when anyone said / roll over, roll over / the middleman thought it would be a fine joke / not to roll over when anyone spoke / but in the struggle he got his back broke / roll over, roll over."

Only the school kids and a few adults are left for the story and swim. The night is as dark as it will get.

"Claws," Helen whispers when my father skips a stone.

"Shush," I say, but squeal when she pinches my arm.

"Nobody move. Hold your breath. Don't even swallow," my father says in the spooky voice he uses to read aloud Edgar Allan Poe tales. "I don't need a stethoscope to hear the telltale empty gut of Big Red churning."

Helen and I shudder in delicious anticipation of being scared out of our wits. It isn't a sequel about an orangutan in the Rue Morgue of far-off Paris my father's going to tell. Big Red is the prehistoric monster crab that was frozen alive under the glacier and is nurtured by the human and animal waste we allow to drain into our lake.

"Sugar and spice and everything nice, like snakes and snails and puppy dog tails, that's what Big Red craves to feast on tonight," my father says. "He's hungry enough to digest the amputated claws of his freshwater relatives."

Helen and I cross our hands over our necklaces so the claws won't click and attract the ancient crustacean. Lily didn't mention that danger when she made us crayfish claw necklaces the summer she spent at the lake.

"Girls who wear pearls shed tears," Lily told Helen. "Crawdad claws clasp a sweetheart fast."

A black cloud blots out the stars and is reflected in the lake. Helen and I lift our necklaces and drop them under the sweatshirts we're wearing over our bathing suits.

My father says, "Nights like this, when he roams the lake searching for prey, Big Red waves his bailer and swimmerets back and forth, causing a swirling current. It's visible from a raft, boat, pier or, most dangerously, from the shore. Do you see any ripples?"

"A few, maybe, Uncle Al," Helen says.

Kenny and cousin Bob shout, "Nazi sub, torpedoes!" And make the sounds of machine guns, explosions, sirens, and then drop to the stony shore in flailing death throes.

"I don't see a thing," I say.

My father thrusts his hand toward me and snaps his fingers. "Be alert," he says. "Keep your eyes wide open. Big Red does. His stalked, compound eyes keep a sentry-watch for food and danger. If he's threatened, he darts backwards to the safety of his lair under the huge Rock of Ages the glacier left. But he can grow another eye, or mandible, or antenna at his next moulting time. He waits. The water blackens above him as he moves to the shallows for a midnight feast. Hey! Like that patch over there – see it? That big black area the size of four main beach rafts? He's not fussy. He *snatches* you in his giant *pincers*, dead or alive, human or otherwise. *Tears* his victims apart, slowly *kneads* and *crushes* each piece with his jaws clamped shut. *Sucks* the mangled morsels down his short esophagus, and *chews* the bits with three movable horn-like teeth in his stomach. A sieve of fine bristles at the bottom of his gut lets only the finest particles enter his filter pouch. They move through it in a fluid stream into the ducts of his large digestive glands. Heads, heavy bones, anything too large or hard is *funnelled* into his intestine to be eliminated or regurgitated."

Somebody makes vomiting sounds in the silence.

My father waits until the gagging ends before he asks, "When do yesterday, today and tomorrow become one entity?"

"Midnight," Helen and I answer.

To which he replies, "Ah, yes, my darling mortals. To discombobulate Shakespeare's A *Midsummer Night's Dream*, 'when the iron tongue of midnight hath told twelve,' and Katepwa's nightmare gorilla crab is desperate. Don't sit on the pier and dangle your legs in the water or dive into the lake to swim if Big Red's claws roil the water."

"Race y'all in," I yell, peeling off my sweatshirt. Claws tickle my chest. "Last kid in's crabmeat," I call as I sprint to the end of the pier while my father dives in without a splash and surfaces swimming.

I skim the lake's surface in the same long, smooth, racing dive as his and do a high-speed Australian crawl as graceful as

Helen's out to deep water where my father is doing the dead man's float.

I'm too young to be afraid of anything when I'm within reach of my father.

I don't yet know the Latin word for crab is cancer.

Here and now? Fifty-three years later, I can hear my father quote Henry Austin Dobson's *Paradox of Time*: "Time goes, you say? Ah no./Alas, Time stays, we go."

Today is Friday, July 1, 1994, and we're at the lake to celebrate. A horde of family members, including my sister Heather and her husband John Verhoeven, are here. Eleven of us will be seated at the long pine table, and two will sit under it - our Terripoo Scottie and Judy and Alexis's Schnauzer Kayla - a lucky separation that avoids setting thirteen places.

"Nearly the whole fam-damily," Mother says as she sets the table, a job she loves. She's especially pleased Heather and John are here this year. So am I.

"Like the fifties," I say when Heather comes into the kitchen to help me make a platter of sandwiches.

"Except we aren't stuck here all week without a car," Heather says. "It's great Frank could come this Friday."

Earlier this morning I craved the special Saturday lunch I treat myself to when I need my childhood comfort food: a bowl of vanilla ice cream and a toasted white bread sandwich of peanut butter and lettuce. Via ESP, I heard Lily whisper: "Friday seem like Saturday, kin going to die." I looked at Frank, and decided to make egg salad sandwiches for lunch like his mom used to make for him to eat Friday nights on his way down here for the weekend.

In the fifties, the three children and I, and whatever leaping dog we had, did the Bear Hug Polka with Frank as soon as he got out of the car. Too long gone, I'd murmur to Frank that night in bed, fondling as if time lost was found.

When Frank was reading the children bedtime stories, Heather and the girlfriend she had at the lake with her, most often Joanne, would come into the cottage from their sleeping porch to greet him before they disappeared until noon Saturday. One of their adventures was to walk a mile down the road to the cottage on the crest of Thrill Hill and spy on some boys their age who played strip poker Friday nights. What time they got home and sneaked into their sleeping porch thirty feet from the cottage was unknown to a couple of early birds in dreamland.

Our first born, Judy, was six months old and Heather was twelve in 1952 when we began spending July and August at the lake. Mother's summer holiday was to stay in Regina and work at her part-time job on the information desk at the Medical Arts Clinic. She came out to the lake Saturday afternoons and went back Sunday evenings.

After Heather went to university in Saskatoon at the end of the fifties, she wrote to tell Mother she'd met a guy named John Verhoeven from Tuffnell, Saskatchewan, who was really nice, as nice as Frank; the only problem was he was really old, almost as old as Pat.

John was as handsome as Frank too, Mother and I agreed when we met him. And he and Frank hit it off like old friends. Heather and John decided to get married the way Frank and I had, no fuss or guests, just the two of them. The date they picked was Wednesday, January 16, 1959. Then Gran Sophie died unexpectedly and her funeral had to be held that day.

Mother told Heather and John it was bad luck to cancel a wedding to attend a funeral, and they should go ahead with their plans. In June, Frank was the MC and Mother and I were head table guests at a barn dance and dinner John's parents held at their farm. For thirty-four years we've talked about how much fun it was to beat our feet on the barn's new floor faster than the dulcimer's hammers hit its strings.

That isn't something we discuss today. We all know this might be Frank's last July 1st.

Our three daughters arranged for today to be a Father's Day encore. Alexis made the banner above the front door that says: TO THE BEST GRANDFATHER IN THE WHOLE WIDE WORLD. Kathy and Heather brought hors d'oeuvres and an angel food cake dessert, Judy and Barb the French bread, potatoes ready to bake, and salad fixings. John, who bought the steaks he'll barbecue if Frank's not up to it, is outside now, setting up the hoops for the Eyeball Senior Croquet Challenge this afternoon.

Mother and Frank are sitting in the pair of steel Plantation rocking chairs that we had on our porch in Tuscaloosa. Glancing up at the two of them, I'm struck by how much my husband looks like my father. The stationary rockers make it safe for Scottie and Kayla to play musical laps, jumping up and down from lap to lap. The Katepwa history book is on my lap open at Mother's reminiscences.

"This is the nicest Dominion Day weather-wise I can remember," Mother says. "Not the breath of a breeze."

"Canada Day, now, Florence." Frank raises his beer mug of Gatorade and taps it against her glass of lemonade.

"How come you didn't even mention July 1st in here, Mother?" I tap the history book.

"I did. July 1st, 1917, the last year of World War One. I was fifteen. It was on a Sunday."

"You didn't date any memories, just gave them headings." I scan *Growing up years*. "This?" I read aloud: "*[I remember]* the *Sunday the pews in the little Anglican church were varnished and the awful ripping sound when everyone stood up – and looked quickly around to be sure nothing had been left behind on the pew.*"

We laugh.

Through the west window behind Mother and Frank, I can see across the glassy lake to the far shore, up to the flat top of the hills and fringe of green flax that will briefly flower the same azure blue as the sky. If my father were still living he'd be almost ninety-four. Frank looks nearly that old when he stops laughing. More than a quarter of a century added to his sixty-seven years by cancer. I shut my eyes and hear my father softly singing: "Hear the wind blow, love/ Hear the wind blow."

A colour photo of our cottage taken by Douglas Walker illustrated an article in *West* magazine about the summer retreats of writers. It shows the stone steps to the front door bathed in the rosy glow visible inside the cottage through the windows. Before he took the photo, Walker turned on all the lights inside and waited outside for the moment the sun slipped down behind the hills across the lake. Gazing at the copy hung over my computer makes me feel as if I'm wrapped in a warm hug.

Thanks to Frank, I'm a connoisseur of the fine arts of a lingering embrace and a quick clinch. How much longer will I be able to nuzzle his neck and feel him lift his chin proudly when I call him my Old Hugger?

As our eldest daughter Judith says in her poem "The Women in the Family," our rituals continue: "After breakfast, the women in the family / take their coffee and sit in the sun / on the wide stone steps... / The women talk incessantly. / Even the ones who aren't there / make their presence felt."

We believe the Qu'Appelle Valley legend that a young Cree brave kept hearing someone call him from the shoreline as he paddled down the lake. "Awina Katepwet?" he called back. "Who calls?" When he arrived at camp, he was told his sweetheart had died calling his name.

The voices call us back each summer. My long-dead father asks, "Why is there never a whole day?" and answers, "Because each day begins by breaking."

But we know, just know, Lake Katepwa is magic. And yesterday, today and tomorrow are one entity in daylight as well as at midnight. No matter what, Frank and I will always be part of this place.

REGINA
About 9 pm, Monday, July 4, 1994

Frank and I have just chosen two photos Judy took on July 1st to put on the fridge. One is of all the croquet players and umpire Scottie, lying stretched out on the close-cropped grass, his front paws crossed, watching. The other photo, my favourite, is of Alexis, her gramps Frank and her great-uncle John standing in a triangle, mallets ready.

It's late, but not dark, when the phone rings. In a high-pitched voice, Heather says, "John went for a bicycle ride after supper and there was an accident and the police are here and they think John might be dead and I don't know what to do –"

"Call 9-1-1 and we'll be right over," I say.

"He's not *here*," she wails.

"Oh shit, oh shit," I repeat while Frank drives the three blocks to their house. Oh shit-shit a shitty short-circuit I always say shoot, I'm useless.

Two policemen are standing inside the front door with Heather. She looks as if she may collapse. It's Frank who takes charge, asking questions as calmly as the policeman answers them. The accident happened on the bicycle path east of the Lewvan Expressway by the ball diamonds. Some young boys riding behind the speeding cyclist witnessed him being violently thrown over the handlebars. He was unconscious and bleeding so they ran across the park to a house and phoned an ambulance. Unfortunately, the first ambulance driver couldn't find the accident scene and one of the ballplayers who gave artificial respiration to the victim had to call again on his cellphone. They don't know for sure who the man is at Pasqua Hospital. He didn't have any ID on him and –

"Oh," Heather says, "John always takes his. Always!"

So it can't be him, I think. It can't.

The other policeman says, "They got Mr. Verhoeven's name at the station by checking bicycle license records. We need a family member to identify whether it's him or not."

Again, it's Frank who speaks up. "We'll go," he says. He puts his arm around Heather and says he thinks she should come too or she might be sorry later, but first he wants to phone John's brother Merv and tell him what happened in case he and his wife Bonnie want to meet us at the Pasqua.

We follow the police car and look straight ahead at its flashing dome light on the Lewvan as we pass the accident area.

Bonnie and Merv are waiting at the Emergency entrance. We hug each other and say "I hope..." before the policemen lead us to the victim's cubicle.

A sheet is over his body, but his face isn't covered.

Heather says, "Oh, poor John. Poor John."

Bonnie says, "He doesn't look like our John."

I say, "Not without that big smile of his."

The policemen turn to Frank.

"Yes," both Frank and Merv say, only, "Yes," nod their heads, cross themselves, and are silent.

John Godfried Verhoeven has that great-to-see-you smile of his in the picture above his obituary. It says he died at sixty-one suddenly and unexpectedly while cycling. It doesn't mention the fact that his elderly father, John, was a prize winning bicycle racer in Holland in his youth.

What if John, the son of a Dutch racer, hadn't been pedalling so fast that evening? What if the boys riding behind John were trying to pass him and he went faster instead of slowing down to let them?

It's a truism that there are more reasons to ask "what-if" about accidental death than when a silent killer inside your body can't be stopped.

Heather doesn't know that our father switched his specialty from pathology because he liked patients to talk to him and it was too late during post-mortems.

When Heather received the coroner's report, it said, "This man arrived at the Pasqua Hospital Emergency in full cardiac arrest. According to police he was bicycling at considerable speed when he fell off the bicycle. He was on the bike path near the Lewvan Expressway. A post-mortem was ordered but no inquest." Listed as the cause of death were atherosclerotic cardiovascular disease, multiple blunt trauma injuries, ruptured liver, hemoperitoneum, multiple fractures of ribs, subcutaneous emphysema, contusions right lung, fracture right clavicle, aspiration of gastric content. The classification: accidental.

What if John could have answered the coroner's questions? Would it help stop the need to ask "what if?"

When Heather phoned the coroner to ask some questions about her report, the coroner told her that "full cardiac arrest" wasn't the cause of his death, it was the result. The coroner added, "Only God knows what happened that day."

What if we believe that's true and it doesn't help a bit?

Maybe, I have to admit, there are worse ways to die than from Frank's cancer. Maybe, I have to accept, "what-if" is a question the living always ask.

But, oh, dear God, John was supposed to be here to help me after Frank dies.

November

November 1994, All Saint's Day, and the death month of both of our fathers from heart attacks. The thirty-fourth birthday of our favourite youngest child in two days is the only happy date Frank has filled in on his master calendar for this month: 3) KATHY BORN 1960; 9) DR. BLAIR DIED 1948; 24) DAD DIED 1959.

While he was recovering from surgery, Frank recorded the memorable dates of each month in a 1991 calendar he labelled: *Family Birthdays & Anniversaries – KEEP*. It's a Canadian Travel Associates calendar that promotes environmental protection with photographs of nature's wonders around the world. November's ice-blue lake and rock wall of snow-capped mountains in Banff National Park look as cold as it is here, but more scenic.

Frank is weak and shaky today, and tricky. He clutches my arm to help me travel safely across the patches of black ice on the parking lot up to the Pasqua Hospital's main entrance.

When one of his knees gives out, he says, "Just doing my hockey hip-hop to show off for my old high school sweetheart."

"Cha Hee, Cha Haw," I reply. "Just doing the Central cheer for my old heartthrob, Silver Blades." But I saw him wince.

Rough ice doesn't bother him. He looks forward to winter, loves it, he says, and plans to cross-country ski again through Wascana Park with his brother Stan in 1995 instead of just walking. Because of Frank's nerves of steel and high threshold of pain, an audience of medical students gave him a standing ovation as the star of his second spinal tap, a notoriously painful bone marrow test. In the weather and chemo comfort zones of September and October, he worked outside putting the garden to bed and battening down the hatches. My pillar of strength, I think, and pull his arm in closer to me. But he needs the Saint Christopher medal he carries in his wallet so he won't fall struggling against the blasts of cold wind. It's a long walk up to the doors. It's a long walk inside, too.

The lab where Frank has his blood test is on the northeast side of the complex, and the cancer clinic is a marathon walk away on the southwest. The main floor of the hospital is undergoing major renovations in this wing. Minor fix ups and the orderly storage of displaced equipment are being ignored. I try to steer Frank to one of the wheelchairs lined up like grocery carts down the hallway beyond the Blood Lab waiting area. He lets go of my arm, stands beside me and sways slightly, leaning from one side to the other for a moment as if he's doing an imitation of the Tower of Pisa, then straightens up and marches stiffly, left-right-left-right, to the lab window to put his name on the list.

I look to see what the signs say today on the curved front of the semicircular counter where patients are admitted to the hospital. The balsawood letters of ADMITTING, repeated four times, have been coming unglued and dropping off. I know it's ridiculous, and I haven't told Frank, but I read the remaining letters as if they're words in a horoscope, and I try to believe that when all the letters have fallen off, Dr. Rayson will tell us Frank's cancer is cured and he's healthy again. In a notebook I carry in my purse, I record what letters are left, but I was so distraught at Frank's condition I forgot the notebook today. I memorize the remaining letters by saying them over and over to myself: MITTING / ADMI TING / AD IN / AD IT IN /.

I repeat the message: *add it in.* Out of the distant past, I hear myself lowball how much of my family allowance cheque I've spent on a Saturday shopping spree, and I hear Frank say to our children, "Your mother can't add, but she sure can multiply." It's an ability I'm currently applying to worrying about Frank.

Frank is sitting in a plastic chair waiting to be called in for his blood test. He's paler than the little white ghost who came to our door last night calling, "Trick or treat," and holding up his Pooh Bear pillow slip for candy. I go over and tell Frank I'm going to the ladies room and, propelled by barely controlled anxiety, take off for the cancer clinic.

I speed-walk through the clinic's public waiting area with its rack of cancer pamphlets, magazines, books, free coffee, fruit juice and oatmeal cookies; go past the reception desk into the treatment area, over to the nurses' station, and halt.

Breathlessly, I let loose with a spiel of questions.

"What could have caused Frank's sudden weakness walking? Did his tolerance for pain hide early symptoms? Will his condition improve? Get worse? Be permanent? Change his prognosis to terminal? Exactly how close is Frank to dying? How long has he got?"

I stop yakking. Take a deep breath. So do the two nurses.

"How long have I got?" was Frank's instant response when he was told he had cancer. Mentally, not physically, I do the rag doll flop, hanging over and dangling my hands near my toes to relax like we did before going on air at CBC Radio. Slowly, I straighten up and answer myself.

I say, "Please excuse that outburst. As a doctor's daughter and mother of four, I know it's medically impossible for anyone to predict the exact time of death or birth. I shouldn't have asked. I'm afraid Frank will try to walk here without me to hang onto and fall so I have to run back and get him for the consultation."

I meet Frank about two-thirds of the way to the clinic. He's not walking fast, but at a steady pace and his shoulders are straight, his chin up, and he's smiling.

Colleen, Frank's chemotherapist and assistant to Dr. Rayson, his oncologist, shows us into the social worker's cheerful office. I brace myself to hear bad news when I see the large box of tissues on the coffee table.

Dr. Rayson is efficient, thorough, exact and friendly. She calls us Pat and Frank – except during a rectal or testicular examination when she dignifies the positions she asks Frank to take by calling him Mr. Krause. I believe my father would approve of the straightforward way she tells us the facts, good and bad, in consultations about Frank's progress.

She sits in one of the chairs in the living room style grouping with us instead of at the desk. We always begin the Saskatchewan way with a comment or question about the weather.

"Sorry to bring you out here on such a miserable day," Dr. Rayson says. "Are we going to get a November snowstorm?"

Frank says, "Wouldn't be the first time. In 1937 when I was ten, I rode my bike from east end Regina to the airport through a Remembrance Day blizzard to see a USSR Lockheed 12. It was grounded on its way to the Arctic to search for the crew of a Russian plane lost near the North Pole on a trail-blazing flight from Moscow to Fairbanks."

"My uncle Bill Wilson was the radio operator on the search plane," I butt in.

"Right," Frank says. "I found out later Bill engineered a radio direction-finding system for keeping in touch with the search plane and to help its navigation." Frank smiles at me. "Pat's uncle also built a transmitter operating on one of the amateur bands so he could exchange messages with his new bride in Toronto – but that's another love story."

Then we get down to business. Dr. Rayson says she has to stop Frank's chemotherapy. The dye-test shows heart damage. The oncologists she consults at the Mayo Clinic agree. There's also evidence of cancerous lymph nodes in his spine.

She doesn't say the spine is a conduit to the brain. I look at the box of tissues. *Add it in,* I tell myself, do not multiply nor dwell on it.

Frank is the first to speak. "That's it for chemo?"

"Yes," Dr. Rayson says.

He says, "In high school, I wanted to join the Air Cadets and get my wings. A bunch of us went to the McCallum Hill Building for our medicals. The first guy examined came back out to the waiting room red as a radish, and whimpered, 'The doc's a lady!' We all flew out of there faster than Flash Gordon and went down to Eleventh Avenue to join the Army Cadets."

Dr. Rayson smiles. I don't. I'm a little embarrassed and very surprised at how Frank is rambling on about flying. Frank doesn't smile either. He looks like he did when he opened the subject of not being kept alive with tubes, wires and pumps by stating what he had to say was "deadly serious."

He leans toward Dr. Rayson. "Getting my wings is the last thing I want to do now, and I'm glad to have a lady doctor to make sure I don't. What's the next step?"

There is no cure for non-Hodgkin's lymphoma. Chemotherapy, radiation and bone marrow transplants are treatments that can lead to a remission of up to ten years. Most deaths occur between six and ten years. Neither one of us asks if the nearly three years since Frank was diagnosed count.

At sixty-seven, Frank is more than two decades too old for a bone-marrow transplant. A Vancouver oncologist Dr. Rayson knows increases his cut-off age for transplants every year on his birthday, but he's still in his forties.

Radiotherapy might stop Frank's malignant white blood cells from multiplying out of control – and it might not.

The pros, cons, procedures and possible adverse reactions are explained to us. Advances have been made in radiation treatment, Dr. Rayson says, advances that my father only dreamt of when he was director of cancer services back in the forties: targeted radiation in high doses, a powerful linear accelerator.

A last chance at whistling past the graveyard, I think – I pray – and smile at Frank. I'm the one who was known by the neighbours as the Hill Avenue Whistler when I was a girl. But oncologists know Frank as a responder to treatment, at least in the short term, and I hope he'll decide to go for it.

On the back of a 1940s high school photo Frank wrote: *Stan is wearing his Air Cadet uniform and I'm wearing my Army Cadet uniform.* Now I know why Frank was a ground cadet fifty years ago and his kid brother Stan was a sky cadet. Earthbound Eye Senior, fly boy Eye Junior. The more we change, the more we stay the same. Still, Frank Ernest is a formidable Big C fighter.

It's quicker to have radiation therapy than the hours it took for chemo, but I wouldn't have time to go home even if it was feasible, which it's not. I drive Frank to a half-hidden south door within steps of Radiation Therapy, help him in on bad days, and do a marathon from and to the car parked on a gravel lot.

Frank's lymph nodes are mapped with an indelible ink needle. The marks won't wash off in the shower and he calls them his "Big C tattoos." It takes a lot longer to position the linear accelerator on the exact spots than the few seconds it does to zap each one.

Seeing the curious display of a half dozen face masks of clear plastic through the hallway window of the Mould Lab is what first drew me in to ask what they were and why they were hanging on the wall.

While I wait for Frank, I talk to Wanda who makes the head masks. Her majors at the University of Regina were visual arts and psychology. The masks are designed to prevent the patients they're moulded on from moving their heads one iota during radiotherapy. Frank doesn't need one because he isn't having radiation on his head.

The forms are made by first applying alginate (a rubbery gel like dentists use for impressions) over the patient's head, neck, ears and closed eyes, leaving only the nostrils free to breathe, then covering the gel with plaster of Paris. The bump of a tiny mole, a dimple, even a mark from acne or chicken pox is reproduced on the final clear plastic mask made from the form.

The head masks are such exact replicas that it's easy to recognize to whom each one belongs. So only the first name or nickname of the patient has to be used on the identification sticker under each of the half-dozen masks hung on the pegboard. For patients concerned with privacy, which some still are about having cancer or being considered a cancer *victim*, their last name spelled backwards is used to identify their mask.

Wanda says, "Historically, people have worn masks in dances for rain or bountiful harvests, as disguises in operas, plays, movies, comics, literary books – and to cure the sick."

"Like the masks the surgeon and nurses wear in the operating room and yours for radiation patients," I say.

Wanda looks up at the masks, and says, "Even masks that expose instead of hiding work if you know why they're used."

"Or nobody knows it's a mask," I say. "My husband Frank once painted on a black eye to wear to a costume party as a subtle protest against costumes. He said he didn't know why it was out of style to invite your friends to come to a party as who they are. It seemed as if every party we went to was a costume party: Roaring Twenties; Hawaiian; Mafia Dons & Molls. It was at the 1940s High School Daze that he blacked his eye and enjoyed having everyone call him Eyeball, his high school nickname. Nobody knew his shiner was shoe polish."

"He knew," Wanda says. "Masks define the roles people play, or the other way around."

"Halloween Twosomes was the theme of the last big party that broke the costume trend. Frank and I went dressed in one costume as Siamese twins and our best friends, John and Betty Stein, went as a pair of dice, their torsos enclosed in big boxes painted white with black dots.

"It took a lot of sewing and Rit dye to make our two-armed and three-legged costume. Our top was two of Frank's old shirts sewn together where I cut off the left sleeve of one and the right of the other, and dyed them orange. I sewed big clownish buttons on the new front seam and name tags under our collars identifying Frank as Tweedledum and me Tweedledee. Frank's dad was our babysitter and he helped us get dressed by doing up the original shirt buttons at our backs. Our pants were his-and-her cords sewn together with a doublewide centre leg and dyed purple. We tied our right and left legs together three-legged style and made our two feet look like one in a homemade felt boot. We had to get rhythm to spud-walk several blocks to the party."

"And for masks?" Wanda asks.

"I can't remember if I made or bought the yellow cardboard coolie hats we wore. The false noses and moustaches attached to eyeglass rims were from the Metropolitan five-and-dime store on Eleventh Avenue. I still have some of that costume somewhere thirty-five years later. The Krause Twins and the Stein Dice tied for the trick-and-treat first prize of witches' brew boilermakers in large pickle jars inside pumpkins. Frank had to un-twin himself for a bathroom break after we drank them and, for the rest of the party, I was left dangling his empty costume, half of me gone."

"Sounds as if you've thought about that costume recently," Wanda says after a few moments of silence. "I don't mean to pry, but are you in counselling? Or are you a nurse?"

I laugh, and say, "No, to both, and sorry for laughing. I'll tell you why I did sometime. What you do and what you know about masks fascinates me."

I want to tell Wanda about the elderly couple still living in their huge three-storey house and sharing a double bed in a bedroom with closets full of Roaring Twenties clothes. How the man propped the woman up in a pillowed nest on her side of the bed and she helped us choose clothes to try on and model for her approval. For Frank: a tuxedo so expertly tailored it was futuristic – and black patent leather Fred Astaire dancing shoes. For me: a satin-lined maroon velvet butterfly cape, gold kid button shoes handmade in New York, and a dropped-waist gossamer dress with beaded bodice and swishy 23-skidoo skirt. For us both: the accessories and jewellery to make us picture-perfect. I want to tell Wanda we needed a butler and chauffeur to carry our Bonwit & Teller and Sachs boxes to our limousine.

Next time.

I go back to Therapy to see if Frank is ready and "pat-waiting" – his double entendre abbreviation for "Patiently waiting" that he says he's a pro at and I agree.

Today, for the first time ever, he needs me to finish doing up the buttons of his flannel shirt. As I slip them in the button-holes, I can't help thinking of the trouble his father had doing up the shirt buttons of our Siamese twins' costumes. It was symptomatic of a bad heart as we learned three weeks later after he died of a heart attack. I sense that Frank is remembering this too. When I finish, he puts his hands on my cheeks, purses my lips, and kisses them – another first.

I take Frank to the Mould Lab on the way out to see the masks hung on the wall like art.

"What happens to the masks after patients are well again and don't need any more treatments?" he asks Wanda.

"They get to take them home with them," she says.

"You should have a mask made so I can see through you," I tell Frank.

"You already do," he tells me.

Yes, and I know we're both hoping that he'll be able to record November 30th on his KEEP-calendar: *Big C cured!*

Tragedies

When Frank's brother Stan drops off his mementos of the Trans-Canada Airlines disaster over Moose Jaw, I'm transported back more than forty years to the day of the crash.

I hear the radio reports again, see the headlines, feel the words pile up and blacken that bright sunny Thursday morning of April 8, 1954: *Crippled passenger plane wafted down like a leaf, bodies dropping to earth from it. Crashed a few hundred feet from Ross Elementary School filled with pupils. Wing ripped off TCA North Star lands on the golf course. House airliner hit exploded in inferno of flames. Grisly remains strewn everywhere, witnesses in shock; a child found an air stewardess's cap lying undamaged in debris on the ground.*

I shudder, and try not to imagine the scene of another, even worse TCA disaster that occurred two and a half years later. Fate and a birthday let Frank think of that crash as a near-death experience; he always bows his head in a moment of silence on its anniversary. In Moose Jaw, as one of the TCA officials who helped the police identify bodies, Frank was near death for many days. Stan's involvement was unknown to me until today.

174

The brotherly exchange of their TCA past began last Sunday when Frank gave Stan a copy of the professionally taken group photograph of the 1954 TCA staff Christmas party. On the photo, from a memory I envy, Frank had written the names of all forty-six partygoers, including the easy ones of recently hired TCA Ramp Agent Stan and his wife Guzz – a childhood nickname that stuck instead of Ellen, her given name. It was fun to see how young we were forty Decembers ago and gossip about what had happened to everyone since then.

In return, this Sunday after Mass, Stan brought over his collection of newspaper clippings and box of snapshots he took less than two hours after the Harvard trainer hit the TCA North Star six-thousand feet above Moose Jaw. I suspect Frank never knew that Stan and his co-worker Ken had driven to Moose Jaw in a TCA truck that morning. Both Sales and Operations employees were trained in the emergency rules for carrying out their duties in the case of accidents. Panel trucks had to be used as hearses in Moose Jaw after the crash. The red maple leaf logo on the TCA truck, and on Stan and Ken's jackets along with their ID tags, would have given them access to areas closed to onlookers.

I'm not looking forward to a Sunday afternoon sightseeing trip through the words and pictures of sudden death. But, at this stage of our pilgrimage together, I guess it's easier to look back at that deadly event in Moose Jaw than to look any farther into our future beyond the precarious security of now.

Frank says, "The trick to looking ahead is to avoid taking a cloverleaf exit to a turnpike that leads to a dead end."

That's one of his maxims for living with cancer. It's a phrase he coined trying to bypass Kansas City, Missouri, on our October 1989 car trip to Tuscaloosa for the one-hundreth birthday of my southern Episcopalian godmother Ormie, a no-nonsense suffragette.

Today is December 4, 1994, the second Sunday of Advent. In five days we'll celebrate our daughter Barbara's 1955 birth at 4 a.m. on December 9th. Oh, how I'd wanted her to be born a day earlier so I could piously joke that her birthdate was on the Feast of Immaculate Conception nine months after I became a Roman Catholic convert. Thank God she stayed put in my womb until the 9th. "Born on the right date to save my life in 1956," Frank says every year on her birthday, and gives her a hug.

Now that Frank's radiotherapy is kaput, instead of me driving him five miles to the cancer clinic on weekdays, I drive us five blocks to St. Anne's Church for the 6:30 a.m. Mass. He always says I don't need to go with him – that the walk will do him good – and uses a riff of flattery to let me off the hook.

For example, he says, "Sleep in if you want, hon. Looks like you've had your beauty sleep, though." He cups my face in his hands, tries to gaze at me adoringly doing his glass-eye trick, gives me an air-kiss, and says, "So don't get up and ruin the reputation you boast about as an unruly convert."

But of course I get up, cheerfully. I know how important it is to him. But he's not a fanatic. He says attending Mass does for him what a Tuscaloosa shoemaker promises to do on his sign: We heel the sick/Restore the sole/Take care of the dyeing.

True, sometimes I brag that I'm the exception to the rule that converts are the best Catholics. But I did take lessons, which Frank took with me to renew his faith. We know that in the canon of the Roman Catholic Mass, *Memento* – with an upper case M – is either of two prayers, one for the living and one for the dead.

Birth and death: December is our Memento month for both. Frank and I sit side by side at the dining room table to look at Stan's memorabilia. Once again, Frank recalls how he got the awful news.

"The westbound DC-3 milk run had been gone about ten minutes when the emergency phone under the counter rang. Bill, the radio operator in the tower, said, 'Frank, one of your planes just got hit over Moose Jaw,' and hung up. While I dialled the downtown office, I thought of the nice couple I'd just checked in on the DC-3. They hoped to be in Calgary on time to connect to Vancouver for a golfing sabbatical on the 'green greens of paradise.' When I heard it was the Flight 9 North Star from Dorval, Montreal to Winnipeg and Calgary that crashed, for a split second I was glad it wasn't the couple's DC-3. Then, I felt guilty. Because so many others had died."

Stan's newspaper clippings are exceptionally well-preserved. They're filed in batches, chronologically, between the pages of the July 1954 magazine *Photoplay* – "Favourite Of America's Moviegoers For Over Forty Years." The photo on the missing cover is described inside as being, "Doris Day, star of Warner Brothers' *Lucky Me*."

A front-page headline in the *Moose Jaw Times-Herald* states: Worst Commercial Airline Crash In Canadian History - Death Toll 37.

The names of the dead listed are of the TCA North Star crew of four – pilot, co-pilot, stewardess and steward – the NATO student pilot of the Harvard trainer from Scotland, and the Moose Jaw woman killed on the ground. But nowhere in Stan's newspaper clippings did I see a name for any of the thirty-one passengers who died.

Frank reads my thoughts. "It took us so long to double-check the manifest, notify all the bereaved next of kin, arrange their flights out here..." He shakes his head. "Releasing the names of passengers is a privacy issue in case...."

I keep my mouth closed and finish his sentence in my mind: in case...the lover a man or woman is flying away from home with isn't his wife or her husband.

Frank doesn't need to remind me of the long days he spent driving grieving relatives and friends from the Regina airport to Moose Jaw and guiding them through the process of identifying loved ones. Frank didn't complain and I didn't ask questions, but some things were obvious. The morgue in the Moose Jaw Armoury must have been as cold as January because after the first day Frank wore his winter coat and at night in bed his normally warm feet were like frozen fish. "All the bodies are shoeless," he murmured half asleep one night. He told me the voices in the Armoury were hushed, choked, or as hollow and faint as echoes, except for an occasional quickly muffled wail. He took my left hand in his, rubbed my wedding ring, and said a brother was only able to identify his sister's remains by the inscribed wedding ring on her finger. He said he could still hear the sharp bangs of steel heel-guards on military and police boots hitting cement. They kept him awake.

Night after night, Frank dragged himself into the house after the children were asleep, picked at his food, and came to bed with Vick's Vaporub dabbed on his nostrils to get rid of the scorched smell. For days, my twenty-seven-year-old husband was as pale and wan as he sometimes is now at sixty-seven, fighting cancer.

The Sunday after the crash was Frank's last fourteen-hour day helping identify remains and arranging for them to be flown east or west to be buried or cremated. I knew then, know now, the comfort he got, and gets, attending Mass.

After I remove clippings for Frank to read, I scan the ads in *Photoplay*. It's easy to see the fifties buyers of the magazine were females: *Bobbi Pin-Curl Permanent $1.50 plus tax; Debra Paget uses Lustre-Creme Shampoo; Playtex Living Panty Brief; Betty's gay on those days with* MIDOL; *Angel Face by Pond's Cold Cream*... Did this issue sell out to fans of the popular comic team wanting the answer to the question: *Are Martin and Lewis Breaking Up?*

Among Stan's two-dozen snapshots I glance at before handing them to Frank are ones labelled: *Arched front doorframe and steps of demolished house; Part of fuselage beside charred hearse that was parked in the backyard; Wing section on Willowdale Golf Course.*

Frank says, "The starboard navigation light of the Harvard was found embedded in our North Star's port wing."

There isn't a picture of the stewardess's cap. The child probably took it as a souvenir. Was the stewardess hired before 1950, I wonder, when she had to be an unmarried registered nurse?

On April 8, 1954, Frank and I had been married four years, he'd been a TCA Passenger Agent four years, and we were a family of four with two children, a girl and a boy under three years old. By the end of April, it would be four months since we'd become owners of one of the dozen three-bedroom bungalows built by Champ Construction in the gumbo of new Lakeview where the Big Wheels in high school once parked to drink beer.

There we were, the happy young couple with Gerber calendar girl Judy, who was two years and four months old and read A.A. Milne's Christopher Robin verses aloud from memory to her ten-month-old acrobatic brother Jimmy. He'd skipped the crawling stage and just got up and run a few months earlier. Still wearing diapers and a long white flannelette nightgown, he looked like a high-speed Sweet Pea in the Popeye comics.

We didn't have our own dog yet. Spike, the clever dachshund, who rolled back a ball with his nose when someone rolled it to him, was a frequent long-term house guest. His permanent home was with the travelling Electrolux manager Ab Coyne and his wife Audrey on Albert Street. They used to live across the corner from my family home on the former edge of old Lakeview. In 1954, in rainy weather, they'd let us park our car and store our rubber boots at their house to wear walking the two blocks home.

Now, in 1994, after forty-four years of marriage, Frank and I are on the same wavelength. He leans over, pats Scottie, and says, "We'll have to teach you to play rug ball with your nose."

Then we get into one of those old married couple skits where less said would be silence.

"Gumbo," I say.

"Planting potatoes breaks it up," he replies.

"Wooden sidewalks, gravel road, muddy yards and lane."

"Homesteading, hon." He puts his arm around me. "Wasn't it fun? Aren't you glad we were young and you looked so cute in rubber boots?"

"Why did our neighbour calculate the average age of death in the obits every night and refuse to lie down and go to sleep if it was near his age – thirty-three?"

"Be prepared. C'est la vie, love."

I smile at him. "Sabotage blamer."

"Rosemary, our cleaning lady who was paranoid about Soviet spies, the KGB and our 'communist' International Harvester fridge causing the Moose Jaw collision. She wrote me that long letter."

I say, "I wish I hadn't lost it. Maybe we could make sense of it now. All that itty-bitty feathery writing slanted sideways up the pages from a giant woman over six feet tall, with a wrestler's muscles bulging from her big-boned frame. She showed up more than once after the Moose Jaw tragedy and took pictures of our house, but she never came to clean again after the accident."

Frank says, "October 1954."

I say, "Lonely."

"For?"

I pantomime puzzlement. I don't want Frank to know how vulnerable I felt left by myself with the responsibility of caring for two little children. And I don't want to think about what almost happened in December of 1956 when I had three children to look after.

"Remember me?" Frank straightens his shoulders, pushes up the knot on his non-existent tie, and gets down to business. "I'm your guy Eyeball, back from that three-week management course at St. Agathe, Quebec. I was climbing Laurentian mountains of ideas in group sessions on sales plans and how to streamline reservations and ticketing methods. Yeah, taking the first hops on the skyway to retiring as Air Canada district manager in Saskatchewan. The lover who brought you brown and olive green oval casseroles and two matching serving dishes."

"Didn't I thank you?"

"Not till we went to bed forty years ago."

This time, the silence that ends our word association game is filled with bed-bouncing action in the Memory Man's thoughts.

I know Frank knows I made a bargain with God. If Frank came home from St. Agathe safe and sound, I'd become a Roman Catholic. And, thanks to my coffee klatch Catholic neighbours who babysat – Ellie, wife of the obit-mathematician next door, and Helen, across the street – I was able to prove I was serious by taking the two introductory lessons while Frank was away. God kept His part of our bargain. I wish I'd expanded my deal with Him before the 1956 air disaster to bring others home safely too.

D evout converts still come up to me and say, "I remember you! You took lessons when I did at Sacred Heart Church and asked all those questions."

Yes, I did. I asked Father Mooney why the service was in Latin, a root language nobody in Canada spoke except priests; why the choir was at the back of the church and the congregation counted beads instead of singing hymns with them. I wanted to know why Roman Catholics couldn't confess directly to God in private like Anglicans instead of going into a dark suffocating little booth and whispering to a priest who was confined in the next closet with his ear pressed to the connecting grill.

Soon after I learned the Latin responses, the Pope switched the Mass to English, the choir was moved to the front of the church, and congregations had to sing along with them. I learned to lip-sync so our watchful parish priest wouldn't catch me committing the venial sin of silence. If things had happened differently in 1956, I would have had a lot more questions for Father Mooney – and for God too. That was the year that Frank used a pass to fly to Vancouver to see the East-West Shrine all-star football game on Saturday, December 8th.

The West won by an easy 30-0 and the best friends of ours Frank was staying with in Mission, friends who'd recently moved there from Regina, threw a big party to celebrate the victory. Frank was more concerned with getting home than having fun. He couldn't coax Betty Lou to stop dancing long enough to find him an alarm clock that worked. He had to dance her from room to room in their split-level house until she discovered an electric Mickey Mouse clock on a shelf of unwrapped Christmas gifts she'd hidden two years earlier from their children – and herself. He had worse trouble convincing his seriously hungover host, Johnny, to get up at the crack of dawn Sunday morning and drive him to Vancouver airport to standby for an already full morning flight in case there was a no-show.

One of the rules for successful trips on passes is to take the first empty seat on a flight toward your destination even if it isn't a direct flight and means making a stopover and waiting to make a connection. Taking unpopular flights that are too early or too late usually increases the number of no-shows. Frank confided to Johnny that he'd never missed one of his children's birthdays and he had a premonition that if he missed this flight, he wouldn't make it home for his daughter Barbara's first birthday. In fact, he thought something awful might happen.

The early flight was boarded when Frank checked at the TCA counter, but the passenger agent said there were three empty seats. If three paying passengers checked in, or three other pass holders with higher priorities, he'd be bumped from the flight.

The agent had just told him how many empty seats there were when three men waving boarding passes went steaming by to the gate. Frank thought he was done for, but only two of them were booked on the direct flight to Regina. Frank got the last seat.

Artist Doug Morton was in the seat beside Frank. They'd met, but reintroduced themselves, and Doug asked why Frank looked so nervous. Frank explained that until the cabin door was closed he could be deplaned if a ticket holder showed up for his seat. No one did.

Frank and Doug had a pleasant flight. Frank only had a carry-on so he didn't have to wait for luggage after they landed in Regina. He walked through the airport to his car without stopping to talk to anyone or knowing how lucky he was.

Trans-Canada Airlines North Star Flight 810, the flight Frank would have taken if he hadn't got that last seat, was reported missing after turning back to Vancouver with engine trouble.

When one of the TCA agents phoned from the airport to see if Frank was home yet, he answered, and that's what he was told.

Calvin Jones, a twenty-three-year-old guard for the Winnipeg Blue Bombers and one of the few black professional players in Canada, had slept in, and Frank got his seat. About the time we were eating birthday cake in Regina, Calvin Jones was boarding Flight 810, the TCA North Star that would soon go missing. For a long time it seemed as if the plane had simply disappeared. The wreckage wasn't sighted until May 1957 when it was discovered near the top of Mount Slesse – five months after the plane had dropped off the radar. The death toll of 62 made it the worst air disaster in Canada's history. Because of the dangerous mountain terrain, no attempts were made to retrieve the bodies. The plane hit less than one-hundred feet below the hooked peak of Mount Slesse. *Slesse* is Salish for *fang* and locally, the mountain is known as The Fang.

There were two-hundred-mile-per-hour tailwinds that day, and the pilot probably could have made it to Calgary with one engine out if he'd been willing to take a chance. But he wasn't. All the TCA employees said he was the most careful pilot, and the safest to fly with, of any they knew.

The crash remains Western Canada's worst aviation disaster, the sixth most catastrophic loss of life in the history of Canadian flight. The accident that took Calvin Jones instead of my husband devastated the Saskatchewan Roughriders for years because four of the team's best players died in the crash – Mel Becket, Mario DeMarco, Ray Syrnyk and Gordon Sturtridge.

I can remember standing beside Frank at the Roughriders' first football game of 1957 and wondering what he felt when the fans were asked to stand for a moment of silence and the names of the dead players were announced – including that of Calvin Jones. It seemed much longer than a moment. Afterwards, Frank squeezed my hand tighter than usual, and whispered, "That's one moment of silence that's too personal for comfort. But it sure is heartfelt."

During the long silence before that football game I'd said another prayer to thank the Lord for bringing Frank safely home to me.

And at 10 a.m. Mass today, I prayed to God to answer some of the questions I've been saving. Did He protect Frank from a plane crash in 1956 just to let him die of cancer now? Do things really happen in threes, and is this stage of Frank's cancer just another near-death scare? Or are we doing the last lap on the fourth loop of our lucky cloverleaf?

Does a circle close the future out when the past catches up? I have a lot of questions, and only God knows what's ahead for us.

Shadow Dance

The chest of drawers across the room from the foot of our bed is my podium. A copy of the eulogy our friend John Stein gave four years ago for his father-in-law, Allan Larmour, is on it. John's secretary faxed it from Calgary on Saturday as a sample of the kind of things he'll say about Frank's life.

My back is to Frank, but I can see him in the dresser's arched mirror. He's lying on the bed, propped up on pillows, waiting for me to start reading. He can see me in the mirror looking at him. I smile. So does he.

"Don't forget, hon, wherever I go, here I am," he says. He does his signature eyeball roll, shuts his eyelids slowly, one at a time, and folds his hands on his chest.

That's how he dozes on airplanes if we're bumped up to first class and he can put his seat back without crowding the person sitting behind him. Drowsing, he's the young pilot of an Air Canada supersonic airliner deadheading home as a passenger and hero to the Airbus crew. Awake, he's a courteous TCA/Air Canada retiree with thirty-three years and three months of ground service in management. Now, he's thinking, gathering his thoughts.

He looks relaxed, yet businesslike. Blue cotton pyjama top as neat and unwrinkled as the crisp white shirt he always wore under his navy blazer to travel. All that's missing is his newest red paisley tie properly knotted, never loosened even on long overnight holiday flights when our children were young and we hitchhiked to Europe with them on passes. Sitting up straight, head against the blue quilted patchwork day-pillow, his hair looks like a child's drawing of a cumulus cloud, the part straight as a knife. Face shining and cleanly shaved by him this morning at the vanity in the alcove of our bedroom. Then, our positions were reversed. I sat on the bed and watched him standing in front of the mirror over the basin. The seat of his pyjama pants hung as flat as a flap. No more cute buns for me to pat. He said he never thought it would be a treat to do something as mundane as shave. His face looked polished and surprisingly youthful for a man en route to his final destination. Smooth as a baby's bum, he said, and rubbed his cheek against mine. The scent of Aqua Velva is still there.

The corners of Frank's mouth rise slightly in a beatific smile and he wiggles his ears to signal he's patiently waiting.

I have a deep voice that I know how to project from raising four children on the windy prairie, and from speaking to my mother when she has her deaf ear toward me. I lean closer to the mirror and repeat an old tongue twister of my father's that I used as a sibilance test when I worked as a CBC Radio broadcaster.

"I saw Esaw kissing Kate / The fact is we all three saw / For Esaw saw that Kate saw me / And Kate saw I saw Esaw." No spit on the glass. I lean closer and just to make sure I'm ready, say, "Seven, seven, seven. Success, success, success-sss."

The large type in caps and triple spacing make the eulogy as easy to read as a radio script. My hands are a bit shaky as I turn the pages, but my voice isn't. It's steady and sure as I read about Allan's birth and childhood and youthful endeavours. It begins to waver a bit as I start page four.

THE BANK OF MONTREAL TRANSFERRED ALLAN FROM WYNYARD TO EASTEND, SASKATCHEWAN, AND THERE HE MET IDA.

IDA WAS A CLERK WITH THE ROYAL BANK. SHE IMMEDIATELY NOTICED THE HANDSOME NEW BANK CLERK AT THE BANK OF MONTREAL.

AT THAT TIME – THIS IS BEFORE THE BANK OF CANADA AND ITS CLEAR-ING-HOUSE ACTIVITIES – IT WAS NECESSARY FOR BANKS TO EXCHANGE NOTES EACH DAY AND SETTLE UP.

IDA HAD TO TAKE THE NOTES FROM THE ROYAL BANK TO THE BANK OF MONTREAL EACH DAY. WHEN SHE DID THIS, SHE HAD TO CARRY A REVOLVER. CAN YOU IMAGINE A GUN-TOTING IDA?

IT WAS DURING ONE OF THESE EXCHANGES THAT ALLAN SLIPPED HER A BLANK CHEQUE. IT CONTAINED AN INVITATION TO ATTEND THE MOVIES WITH HIM. IDA STILL HAS THIS CHEQUE.

FROM THIS BEGINNING, BLOSSOMED A ROMANCE THAT CONTINUED FOR OVER SIXTY YEARS AND...."

I clear my throat, take the tissue from the sleeve of my sweat-shirt and blow my nose, but I'm unable to read "...WILL CONTINUE FOR ETERNITY."

Through a blur, I see my father's tiny, almost illegible, prescription scribble in a notebook he kept when he was studying to be a doctor at the University of Saskatchewan and McGill:

What is it?
Can any reader by way of a little diversion from domestic
worries or national anxieties decipher this enigma?
The beginning of eternity, the end of time and space,
the beginning of every end, and the end of every place.

I try clearing my throat again.

Frank says, "That's okay. Just let John in on how you chased me until I turned around and caught you. He's a good Supreme Court lawyer. He'll extol me to the heavens so I'm not bumped in purgatory. Don't worry. I plan to stick around for your sixty-fifth birthday Thursday. Having my old gal-pal as my nurse is something to die for that I can live with. I promise to be here, hon."

In the margin of the eulogy beside ETERNITY, I write: *Frank is dying well. Is that an enigma or a paradox? Both, I guess.*

A poem by Ryoho, an eighteenth century Japanese writer, describes the roundelay of living well as we shadow dance:

Scooping up the moon
in the washbasin,
and spilling it.

Sometimes, we try to scoop up the thin blade of a new moon with its sharp ends to put back in the sky, and the orchestra plays "Sabre Dance" as we cut to the past when our nurse-patient roles were reversed.

In the fall of 1950, after Frank and I were married, Mrs. Zimmer, our seamstress, sewed me a long white tulle dress that, during fittings, we called my wedding dress. Somewhere there's a snapshot of me standing in front of our decorated Christmas tree modelling it. I don't have to see the picture to remember the details of its design I liked best. It had a faux strapless top that wouldn't slide down my almost flat chest and expose the padded bra I had to wear under it. The full skirt had three puffy tiers and a crinoline lining so it swished and swung if I just moved slowly. At the waist, it had a four-inch-wide bright red taffeta sash. Mrs. Zimmer and I called the sash my Scarlett O'Hara breath-taker.

The first opportunity I had to wear my "wedding dress" was on a Saturday night in December 1950 to the dinner dance at the Hotel Saskatchewan. It was a really big deal to be going to THE HOTEL. My friend Marilyn's father paid $25 a couple for twelve of us to go and celebrate her birthday. We had to dress to the nines, and Frank had to brown bag our mickey of liquor and hide it with the other bottles under the floor-length skirt of the white linen tablecloth.

The Monday edition of the *Regina Leader-Post* reported on its Social News page that Dr. Hector L. Watson and Mrs. Winnifred Claire LaBrish, dinner dance regulars, and six fashionable young couples in the Kramer party, danced every dance. It said that George Fairfield's orchestra with Pat South on piano played all the old and new dance favourites, but it didn't mention one of the pieces was a piano solo. Frank's brother Stan had asked Pat, who'd gone to Central with us and was a good friend, to play Fats Waller's "Honey Hush" and dedicate it to a couple of record breakers, Eyeball Senior and Butterball. Only the people at our table knew whom she meant.

I didn't feel very well or have as much fun as I'd expected. When we got home to our bachelor suite in the Grenfell, I had a hot bath and broke out everywhere in chicken pox.

Our Murphy bed had a horsehair mattress on it that I'd inherited along with a cherrywood bedstead from my great-aunt Janet. We'd covered the mattress ticking with a heavy damask banquet cloth of my grandmother's, a thick cotton bedspread, a pair of matted wool blankets, and two new sheets. It didn't matter. Horsehairs poked up through all of its layers of coverings and it felt as if we were lying on a bed of sharp needles. Although the pain and the itch of the pocks were awful, and Frank said his warranty wasn't up so he could send me back to Mother to be fixed, he turned out to be a tender loving nurse.

Nursing my heart out wasn't my original choice of vocation, as our high school yearbook attests the year I graduated.

In *Ye Flame 1947*, there's a photo beside the write-up of each of 186 grade twelve students. My name is listed with ten others under the heading: CAMERA SHY SENIORS. About me, the yearbook says: *Our star. She thinks up new ways for bothering the teachers every day. Future in Journalism.*

I was a star at asking questions that disrupted classes.

My father used to say I was born asking: "Why?" In his Tuscaloosa album, there's a snapshot of him sitting on the porch steps with a newly arrived me all bundled up on his lap, my mouth wide open howling. Under it, in white ink, he printed as neatly as he did on his black widow spider slides: DADDY DOC AND A SACK OF HOLLER.

The dubious distinction of being the first girl to have chalk hurled at her by our algebra teacher was a result of my naivety. In one of those dead silent moments when he'd just put a problem on the blackboard and was standing glaring around the room for a victim to solve it, I asked the Park's Billiards sharks in the desks behind me why it was a dirty joke for Mr. X-equals-Y to play pocket pool, and not for them when they skipped school to do it.

In French class, I asked what use it would be in my future life to be able to translate the book *Sept d'un coup* to *Seven at one blow*. Mademoiselle Murphy was petite, white-haired, and softly spoken. But the rumour was that a washing machine wringer had left her with a formidable weapon concealed by long sleeves and a black leather glove. She marched to my desk, told the class to count in French, and rapped me on the head seven times with her wooden arm.

Selectively deaf Miss Tingley, the girls' health and phys. ed. instructor, sent me out to do laps around the track to clear my sinuses when I asked her why she always wrote "cold" on gym excuse slips for menstrual cramps.

I think the personality profiles and predictions of futures are uncannily accurate in yearbooks. But, by the time *Ye Flame 1947* came out, I didn't want to go away for the journalism program I had enrolled in down east at Western University. It's easier for a born sack of holler who practised to be a reporter to ask the five-w questions about my reason for changing my mind than it is to answer them.

Who: Eyeball. What: Lust at first sight. Where: Detention Room. When: Grade Nine. Why: So some other girl won't grab him.

The grade twelve photo of Eyeball I'd clipped from *Ye Flame 1945* and had in my locket was proof he was dreamy looking.

And in *Ye Flame 1946*, the year he graduated from Central on the five-year plan and began working full-time as a parts man at International Harvester, it says: *Eyeball attracts feminine glances from all sides. Between designing cars and thinking up puns, he manages to squeeze in a little school work. Future?*

The answer: With me. No question.

I had to break the news to Dad that I'd changed my mind about going away to university in the fall. I wrote a prescription in my diary for how to convince him I was too young and inexperienced to leave home.

Rx: DOC DAD

1. Call him daddy.

2. Use sweet-seventeen guile to make him think it's his idea that I should stay at home in Regina to work for a year and mature.

3. Subtly remind him he wrote in his notebook: *The greatest profession in the world is that of being a father.*

I planned to thank him for always being so willing to listen to my problems and for helping me make wise decisions.

I vowed not to interrupt with groans and sighs and rolling eyes if he got mushy about meeting Mother at the U of S or wince if he played the bagpipes on his nose and then rolled his R's quoting Robbie Burns: "O, my Luve's like a rred rred rose."

I slept in, missed my bus, and Dad was driving me downtown to my summer job when I tried to wheedle my way into delaying university a year until fall '48.

I flattered: "You were right, Daddy, doing office work's a super learning experience. I'm too old to do kid stuff at the beach, delivering newspapers on my bike, and I'm tired of helping Dene wait tables on Sundays and do dishes in her mom's dining room."

I lied: "I'm never bored at Municipal Hail Insurance. The ladies who've worked there since Mother was the summer office girl are sweet as grannies to me even when I make mistakes. They're teaching me the skills and discipline I need to file policies and hail claims and look after heaps of mail twice a day. Maybe earning a monthly salary for a year while I learn to work hard and be a studious adult would be an excellent investment in my future."

I asked: "Do you think eighteen's too old for me to go to university if I wait until 1948, Daddy?"

Of course he didn't. I knew that. He was always going away to study the diagnosis and treatment of cancer at universities and hospitals in New York and Baltimore and Toronto and Montreal. And, with the support of Premier Douglas, he obtained grants for clinic nurses and technicians to go away for courses at leading cancer treatment institutions.

For the moment, at least, my Rx for delay worked. So did I.

I filed, did mail, and filed some more. I beat boredom by plotting how to capture Eyeball forever and daydreaming I'd succeeded. When the young typists I went out for coffee with had to poke me to go, they joked that I was "filing claims of hailstones the size of eyeballs." They got such a kick out of using that line to describe my condition in the fall of 1947, and in the winter and early spring of 1948, it became a special office term for anyone pining dreamy-eyed over a boyfriend.

Being head over heels in love danced the jitterbug with my emotions. I was a lovesick lump in mood indigo when Eyeball didn't phone for a while and a dance-ballerina-dance doing splits and twirls at the end of the rainbow when he called every night. I studied our horoscopes, my sign for Aquarius and his for Pisces – which I pronounced Piss-kiss if I heard rumours that he'd dated his old girlfriend The Vixen again or someone new.

By the middle of July Eyeball Senior was mine. And I sang the new novelty song, "Three Little Fishes," out loud for laughs, and "Till The End Of Time" to myself as our song. I boasted in my diary about the great catch I'd made and hoped my unending hope that I could keep him hooked.

June 21: First day of the happiest summer in my life if it keeps up the way it started. Eyeball hitchhiked down east to buy a car. I sleep with the postcard he wrote me from Windsor under my pillow for good luck. He got a 1937 Ford with a radio and heater. It's cosier than the 1927 Willis-knight convertible he fixed up in '45 and a lot sleeker than the 1928 Whippet sedan he had last summer. He looks so cute driving it and takes such good care of it. Thanks to Dad, I shift without grinding gears when Eyeball lets me drive his cream puff. He's really generous and often loans his car to his brother and father. Too bad every guy in the world isn't as nice as he is; then every girl would know how lucky I am. He told me last night I'm everything he wants a girl to be and I hope this time he'll think that permanently. Oh, what a beauteous life that'll be.

Oh, summer in the city was such a romantic whirl. Rain on the roof of a steamy Ford, the smell of wet pavement, the swinging skid of tires on the soaked gravel road to my house at the end of Hill Avenue. Hot cement sidewalks heated the soles of my spectator pumps and I danced down the street to meet him after work. Heat waves made the whole world look wobbly. Movies, picnics at Boggy Creek, milkshakes and Boston cream pie at the Dutch Mill, moonlight dances and house parties and necking and talking and parting after one more good-night smooch. And work in the morning, bright and early, where I had trouble not nodding off over policies to file and the grannies got miffed over mix-ups. I didn't have time to record anything in my diary for a month.

On July 22 and 28, my one-line diary entries are just reminders to tell Dad before it was too late that I didn't want to go to university. The deadline to cancel and Dad's departure for a month at the lake nearly collided. My mother had been out at the cottage since the end of June sewing name tags on my wardrobe of college girl clothes and bushels of new underwear. While I procrastinated, Western confirmed my registration and acceptance in residence, and a journalism sophomore wrote to say she was my sponsor for the only sorority allowed on campus.

I imagined a tête-à-tête with my father in the peaceful living room. I saw myself enter quietly on the royal red carpet and stand in the soft cathedral light from the trio of arched windows at either end. Dad would turn around from his desk, look up from the book he was reading in his easy chair, or stand facing me in front of the fireplace with his elbows up on the mantle ready to be witty and wise and answer my questions with questions.

"Well, hello young lady," he'd say, and smile. He would have that happy twinkle in his eyes.

But even back in those days I couldn't seem to get my act together until the last moments shoved me hard against the deadline. That's the pressure I was squashed by Thursday, July

29th, the day I was moving to Dene's to bach with the working girls for August. The last chance I had to tell my father my plans in private was going to be when he drove me there.

In the hot car on the five-block drive over to Dene's with my books and clothes, and sweating bullets (not "perspiring" as Mother claimed ladies do), I began with, "Dad?"

"Sounds like you're not sure," he said. "Are you questioning my identity?"

I said, "No," and it all poured out like syrup. "I'm sure I don't want to be a reporter anymore. It would be a waste of money to send me down east to university to be a news hen. I've decided I want to go in training this fall at the Grey Nuns Hospital where you are or at the General Hospital and be a registered nurse."

His snort made me jump. He took his right hand off the wheel and rapped his knuckles on the dashboard as he spoke. "I do not foresee a born sack of holler adopting the nurses' motto: *I see and I am silent.* Every good nurse I've ever worked with has wanted to be a nurse since childhood," he said. "And I've never before heard you express the slightest desire to be a nurse."

I kept quiet and thought: Excuse me, Mr. Alexander Pope, I know why you said fools rush in where angels fear to tread.

"Nursing is a vocation that requires discipline and devotion, sacrifice and skill," Dad said.

"Like filing," I said.

Both hands back on the wheel, Dad did a U-turn in the middle of Rae Street and scraped the tires against the curb before he braked to a neck-snapping stop in front of Dene's.

"Like filing be damned," he said. "As a probationer you'll have to strip badly soiled beds and learn to remake them with the patient in them, empty full bedpans and scrub them clean

with disinfectant, and obey a strict 10 p.m. curfew on the one
Saturday night off you'll get every six weeks during three years of
training. Do the mathematics."

"I know," I said, but I didn't.

"A nurse gets flat feet, varicose veins, bags under her eyes
from working nights, and loses her boyfriend."

He did a brief wailing bagpipes rendition of the overture to
"Full Moon And Empty Arms" that sounded like a dirge, and
then he looked at me long and hard. The corners of his tightly
closed mouth had that little twitch he got holding back a smile
after he'd told a corny joke or posed a ridiculous riddle from his
little black book that everyone in the family knew the answer to.
I was just going to ask him what was so funny when Dene came
out to help me unload all my stuff from the car and carry it into
her house.

Dad tooted the horn and waved as he drove off.

We had our arms full of boxes and couldn't wave back.

What I wrote in my diary the next Thursday night locked in
the bathroom at Dene's house is brief, formal and taut, but it
doesn't hide the confusion of my feelings; it reveals them.

*August 5: My father had a very serious heart attack and he has to
be in the hospital four weeks. I am not going to varsity and am I ever
glad. I can take a good business course as Daddy suggested and be with
Eyeball, too.*

Sitting there on the toilet lid, two of the easy riddles in my
father's notebook chased each other in my head: *Why is there
never a whole day? Each day begins by breaking. What unites by divid-
ing and divides by uniting? Scissors.*

What if I'd wanted to be a nurse from the day I was born and was now an RN? An angel of mercy? Maybe, my loving patient wouldn't be making final arrangements for himself.

Was it only yesterday that John and Betty Stein sat at our bedside to visit with Frank? We reminisced about the good old TCA days – a family affair in more ways than one. They were in Regina for the Saturday evening wedding of John's sister Betsy, a retired TCA/Air Canada passenger agent, who was getting married for the first time to a widower. Then Frank asked John if he would give the eulogy at his funeral. John – lawyer, philosopher, raconteur, Good Samaritan, dear friend – got tears in his eyes, and could only nod.

Oh, hon, you should be able to put things like that on hold forever and a day – or at least until we're in our nineties.

Listen, you're such a considerate patient. Have I told you that? Showed you how much I appreciate it as a novice nurse? Our nephew, Nurse Bob at Plains Hospital, says I'm doing a great job and I'm not on probation as a nurse anymore.

I tell him it's because I love the patient.

Journal Entries

Sometimes, while Frank underwent tests by specialists other than those at the cancer clinic, I jotted notes to myself in the memo book I keep in my purse. Some of the notes I found in a stack of old pages filled with mundane *To Do* things and grocery lists are about coincidences. They're with the notes about home care on my desktop computer in the *My Documents* file folder *Journal Entries*.

Wed., Sept. 9/92

Frank is having a barium x-ray. A lady in a smart business suit goes by the café window with her hair in rollers. It's a bleak, cold, very windy day, but her curls aren't blowing. So far, in spite of chemotherapy, Frank still goes to 1840 Rose Street for regular haircuts at Dennis's barbershop.

Same page, different ink, undated

Frank is seeing an eye specialist. He has a blind spot in his right eye that might be macular degeneration. I'm just thinking about what this could mean, and a man goes by the car with a white cane that he's tapping along the entrance wall to the ophthalmologist's building.

Tues., Apr. 5/94, about 4:10 pm

I was reading Frank's list of pre-med and chemo drugs Activan, Maxeran, Decadron, Vineritine, Metoxantione, Cyclopphosphamide, when I heard Perry Como singing Jo Stafford's 1954 hit "Teach Me Tonight" and saw a pair of old lovers writing LOVE YOU HON across living skies.

Mayday/94

Jackie Kennedy Onassis has died from non-Hodgkin's lymphoma less than five months after it was diagnosed. That's a downer. Frank and I agree her death seems too perfectly scripted to be natural. We read that the cancer had spread to her brain and thought she seemed like the type who would rather lose her life than her mind. And she took a last walk in the park, called her family together, had her favourite books on the bed and the art she liked best in her bedroom. Dr. Rayson says if the cancer had spread to her liver, oncologists could probably predict the time of death within 48 hours. (She has just told us she wants to put Frank on a much stronger chemo recommended by the oncologists they consult with at the Mayo Clinic, who agree with her that he isn't showing enough progress.)

Thurs., Dec. 20/94

Natural causes versus chemical? It's a sticky question. A tube from the tailpipe into the car, the windows rolled up, the heater on full blast, an elderly couple in their sixties snuggled together like teenagers parked in Neckers' Nook behind the

Legislature Building? Or call a veterinarian to give us each one shot to put us gently and quickly to sleep side by side in our own bed? Forget the chemicals and multiple-zap radiation that damage the heart and burn the throat but don't kill cancer.

JANUARY 1995 DECLENSIONS

Palliate, palliative, palliation. To cloak, mitigate, lessen or abate. Palliated, palliator, palliating.

This is worse than learning Latin declensions in high school when we thought it didn't make any sense to waste our time on a dead language.

You and me: to be or not to be.

Pall, [L. pallium, a cloak.] A large cloth thrown over a coffin or a tomb. Pallbearer: one of the friends who'll attend your coffin at your funeral. If I hadn't got caught skipping Latin and been sent to the Detention Room where you were, would you still have turned out to be my guy? Winning your undying love was a wish and a vow when I kept saying, "Veni, vidi, vici," in those days. Now, it's my battle cry against your cancer, [L. the Crab].

Language lessons I don't want to learn.

Sun. night, Jan. 22/95

Damn, oh, dammit. My back aches and I can't remember the right way to lift you. Is this it? My arms scooped under yours? I'm so scared of making a fatal mistake. Was it only this morning that you made it to the bathroom with the help of a cane? Just an hour ago that you sat up by yourself on the edge of the bed to use the bottle?

How tightly can I hold you and not crush your ribs, cut off your ragged breath?

Will I be able to follow orders if you stop breathing? Not try to give you my breath and keep you here? Do what it says on the signs beside the upstairs and downstairs phones?

REMEMBER: If we need to call an ambulance,
DO NOT CALL 911 (they must resuscitate by law)
CALL: 586-0355 - Home Care Nursing

As I undo the clean diaper, you respond to the ratch of the Velcro and say, "'scuse me." Our fingers scramble with your penis. It's as small as a baby's nub. It used to rise instantly to my touch, if it hadn't already sprung up in anticipation of it. I sense we both think this. I withdraw my hand.

"Dinky-dinky-do," you sing in a stage whisper when you have it caught between your thumb and index finger.

I move the mouth of the plastic gooseneck bottle under its little helmet.

"Closer," you say. "It's not a schnozzole."

We wait.

I reassure you that it's okay to void now, that you won't soil anything, not even the diaper. What has always appealed to me about you is how sexily you combine squeaky clean habits and a dirty mind. I've told you that often. Do I tell you again? Urine finally drools silently down the side of the plastic container.

"Good boy, Pete, tube avoided," you say to your penis, and smile. You expect me to groan at your pun, and I do.

Mon., Jan. 23

Frank is asleep again or pretending to be. The oxygen tank is finally hooked up and I'm being given instructions on how 'to look after it when Kathy and Randy arrive after work with a bedside commode. It's rented from SAIL – the upbeat acronym for Saskatchewan Aids to Independent Living.

DOMINUS VOBISCUM. THE LORD BE WITH YOU.

A *lite flammam*. Keep the flame lighted. Let's hear it for the Central motto, two words arched over a burning torch between curved brackets of wheat on the crest. *Alite flammam* for me, we said to each other as we parted, high school sweethearts pretending to be Latin scholars. Keep the flame burning for me.

And we cheered for lucky C-13 at the hockey games where you got your front teeth chipped and cracked and had to have them capped – which you did without any freezing. Cha hee! cha haw! / cha haw, haw, haw! / Rip'em / smear'em / eat'em raw! / We've got the zip, the pep, the thirst / To light the flame / Put Central first!

"You Always Hurt The One You Love" I keen silently to that old Spike Jones Band's cacophony of clashing cymbals, drums banging, whistles shrieking, bells ringing.

Yes, bells ringing. Tolling.

Lifeline

Friday, January 20, 1995.
Frank goes over the checklist with me
and I tick:

✓ Buy double plot for our grave at Riverside
✓ Choose funeral hymns (I won my argument for "O God
Our Help in Ages Past" to be the entrance hymn)
✓ Add phone numbers beside names of pallbearers
(6 bearers, 9 honorary)
✓ Arrange Catholic Women's League lunch and
what to pay them
✓ Make corrections to obit (I hadn't put down that
he'd gone to St. Joseph's Elementary School)

Frank's pretty well bedridden although he manages to come downstairs for supper and stay awake in his chair so we can watch *Are You Being Served?* together just as if everything is normal. We laugh out loud at the characters and the silly situations they get into.

Tonight's show is a repeat we've already seen twice. Frank mutes the sound with the zapper and we talk about those December days in 1948 after my father died when I took December off from Reliance Business School and clerked at Eaton's for the Christmas rush. Frank came over from International Harvester for lunch – and a quick smooch behind a fridge in Appliances when we could get away with it. Ditching Eaton's store detective whom everyone called Dick Tracy wasn't easy. Seeing where he was floor-walking or lurking was a cinch. He added about five inches to his six-foot-plus height by wearing a fedora, and there wasn't a piece of furniture or a fridge in the store tall enough for him to stand behind completely hidden. The buttoned-up and belted spy-style trench coat he wore summer and winter, the flat-footed way he walked slowly around the store, his toes pointed out, his boat-size brogues smacking down on the cement floor, were all a dead giveaway that he was *the* Dick Tracy. He kept Frank and me under surveillance as we wandered through appliances and furniture, hoping for privacy. Every time we stopped to look, we could see Dick Tracy's head turned toward us and knew that his squinting eyes were focussed on us as if he had magnifying spectacles secreted under the turned-down brim of his hat.

There was another spy at Eaton's who wore a fedora. He was a small thin man in a business suit, and on my first day of work I thought he was going to fall through the stairwell railing when he crouched down, hunched his narrow shoulders, stuck his head between two bars and yelled down at us, "Dust, tidy, straighten things up. Look busy, not idle." I said, "Who's that nutty old geezer?" The notions supervisor bowed her head, partially covered her mouth with her hand, and said, "Meet Mr.

Oldfart, the store manager." Timothy Eaton's was not Grace Brothers Department Store.

Watching little old raunchy Mr. Grace and his clerks on TV serve rude customers is fun. It's true that time spent laughing is time spent with the gods – especially when the one laughing with me has been my Greek god since high school.

Saturday, Jan. 21/95

Our eldest daughter Judy and granddaughter Alexis brought Frank a get-well gift today.

"It's a good-as-new Fisher Price nursery monitor we bought at a garage sale," Alexis informs me.

"It smells like alcohol because I disinfected it with Dettol," Judy says after she takes it out of the box.

"If Gran's downstairs in the kitchen, you can tell her what you want her to bring you, Gramps," Alexis tells Frank while she sets up the speaker on his bedside table. "But Gran can't ask what you mean or talk back to you."

Frank snorts. "Great, I should have had one of these for the last forty-five years."

Alexis laughs. "I don't think they were invented in pioneer days, Gramps."

Later, I discover I can hear Frank on the monitor even with the ceiling fan and air-cleaner on. I'm sitting at the kitchen table sipping wine, and having a cigarette, and I can hear Frank breathing as well as if he was sitting beside me. Of course, the damn smoke would be blowing his way and we'd have to change places like we do...*did* in restaurants.

Oh God, here I am: a smoking cussing fingernail-biting old

lady drinking wine all alone except for her little old dog asleep at her feet, her ancient girlhood diary with its pages all tattered and torn lying open in front of her watery eyes.

The sudden sound of Frank's voice startles me and wakes Scottie. "Miss our Saturday dance," he sings, sounding more like Durante than Como. "Couldn't bear it without you..." He coughs. "That's spelled b-a-r-e, sexy. Thought you were coming up to read me some bedtime stories from your old high school diary?"

I nod my head and say I'll be up in a minute – as if he can see and hear me. For a sex-after-seventy documentary that I did in my radio days, I read Simone de Beauvoir's book *Coming Of Age.* I think that's where I read we only become more of what we were as we grow older. Tonight, to prove her theory to myself, and for sentimental reasons, I promised to read Frank what I wrote about him in my diary in the 1940s.

"Here's to Saturday night live," Frank says, and clicks his glass of Gatorade against my glass of wine. We try to coordinate our toast. I just have to raise my glass and take a sip, but he has to put the morphine capsule on his tongue before he takes a mouthful of fluid and quickly tips back his head to swallow. "And a chaser to the gal who played hard to get," he says, and takes another drink.

"She's not here," I say. "Better not be. Where's she hiding?" I pat the rolled comforter between us that protects Frank from being bumped in the night by me. "You're having a bad hallucination. Thought you said you only saw scenes of yourself driving futuristic cars and flying to the moon with me. So who's this Ms. Hard-to-get? What's her problem? Since when is any woman so dumb she won't let you catch her?"

"You forgot to ask where and why." He puts his arm around me. It's so thin I could cry. "Let's talk about where we've been, who we've turned out to be, and why we're here in bed together now. What've you said about me in that book with the broken lock you're holding? Nothing, I'll bet."

"Cut to my 1948 Chase Catch Keep Race," I say, and begin reading:

Feb. 3 to 8: Got my horoscope for this week and the damn thing really works. Haven't heard from or seen Eyeball for three weeks, but I heard The Vixen went out with a new victim instead of with Eyeball last Sat. night. She sure couldn't like Eye very much. Maybe she just wants him hanging around for someone extra. He's a suck if he does it. My horoscope says I should be cautious in any travel during evening hours. Wonder what'll happen if I'm not? Tues. I have to resist all invitations. Hope I get some to resist. Of course if it was Eye I wouldn't anyway. Well, to hell with this noise, he would have phoned me if he ever thought of me. Life's a thorn, oh why was I born is my motto – for a few days anyway.

April 30: Eyeball's been back since that last entry for a sweet if brief encounter. Went out with him and received phone calls for 2 weeks. Guess even the old friendly interest of his is wearing off. Sometimes I think instead of loving him I hate him so much it has me all mixed up. Well, damn it, I haven't given up yet. Someday he'll realize that I'm meant for him and all that sloppy drivel.

May 28: Sat. night at 1 o'clock. I've just gotten back from a hen party. Eyeball's down east looking for a used car. It's sure nice to walk down the street and keep my eyes in their sockets. When he gets

back, I'll be so thin if I follow him sideways he won't be able to see
me. Hope he wants to. Trouble is, like a stupid ass, I told him before
he left how much I like him and that might make me not as inter-
esting to him. Dammit though, he seemed to like me just as much as
I liked him that night. Well, the gal who wins is the gal who thinks
she can, dammit. I think I can, I think I can, I KNOW I can...

I look at Frank. My old hugger is sound asleep, his arm still
around me. "It's okay, honey hush," I whisper. "It's just more of
the same true romance stuff you already know by heart."

Sunday, Jan. 22/95

Frank uses the monitor to call family members one at a time
up to the bedroom to say his goodbyes. Alexis and Frank's
old pooch-pal Scottie stays upstairs while he does it, but across
the hall in my bedroom-office. Not everybody in the family
shares what he said to them.

My "little" sister Heather, who was an eight-year-old pest
when Frank and I got serious about marriage, and now has been
John's widow for more than six months, says, "He told me to
keep being a brat," and bursts into tears.

"Frank says I'm his favourite mother-in-law and I should keep
playing bridge to win for another 93 years," my mother says after
Alexis helps her back downstairs.

Monday, Jan. 23/95

Frank takes his last shower. I want to help him because he's
so shaky, but he says no. We don't mention it, but I know

we're both thinking of the story our neighbour told us about getting into the tub to shower with her husband when he was dying of cancer and the trouble she had getting him out. She wept as she told us. A few weeks before her husband died, he told Frank he'd decided not to have any more treatments.

An oxygen tank is being set up in our bedroom and the technician is giving me instructions on how to look after it when Father John Perry, our parish priest, an advisory board member at the cancer clinic, arrives without warning. I like Father Perry, but I'm afraid I won't do the oxygen right and I'm annoyed at him for insisting he'll wait in the living room to see Frank. Does Father Perry think it's his final chance to give him the Last Rites?

In one of Frank's awake periods early Monday morning, my back aching from bending over our bed, I ask Frank what he thinks about putting a temporary hospital bed from Home Care in our old master bedroom across the hall.

He squeezes my hand, and says, "We wouldn't be able to see the crabapple tree's hoarfrost and spring blossoms."

Tuesday, Jan. 24/95

Today, Frank died. It's Tuesday. His left eye wouldn't stay closed and for a split-moment I thought it was a trick and I should put a penny on it so he'd laugh.

Dr. Ficzycz came and made out the death certificate. He recorded the cause of death as pneumonia and explained to me with a rueful look that he had to put down the "immediate" cause. I said, "Yes. Good," and saw the muscles beside his mouth relax a little. It must be hard for a doctor to let a patient die of something treatable.

Alexis sat beside the bed with Scottie lying at her feet and held her grandpa's hand for a long time. The others went in and sat beside him or stood at the side of the bed for shorter periods. I kept him at home until early afternoon. His left eye never did stay completely closed. "Grandpa's winking," Alexis said.

When the man from the funeral home was zipping up the body bag, I had to ask him to stop when he got to Frank's chest so I could look at his face. I hated watching the zipper being closed over his face. Until that moment it was just a sleeping bag. I followed him when the men carried him downstairs, but as they were going out the door, I had to ask them to wait. I'd forgotten to arrange the autopsy. Oh, God, I never asked Frank or told Dr. Rayson or discussed it with a soul. After I made frantic calls to the cancer clinic and Home Care, Frank went to the Pasqua Hospital morgue in Helmsing's luxurious velvet and leather-lined hearse. I nearly waved as they drove almost without a sound over the packed snow in our driveway.

When I went back upstairs, our daughter Barbara had remade our bed with fresh sheets. I stood in the doorway and looked at our empty bed. Tuesday, I think, today is Tuesday – sounds like Two's day. What did we do yesterday?

How did Father Perry know it would be his final chance to give him the Last Rites? Frank died at 4 a.m. today, Tuesday, January 24th, 1995, two days before my big birthday that he said he wouldn't miss.

But a lifelong promise-keeper winks *auf Wiedersehen*, not goodbye. I promised to detain him when he returns.

Life After Death

OUR FATHERS

The iron tongue of midnight has stuttered to a stop and yesterday, today and tomorrow are one entity.

The last night Frank was in bed beside me, I knew I had to stay alert. Listen to Frank breathe. If he held his breath, murmured or groaned in his sleep, wake him to find out his pain level, and, no matter how low he said it was, coax him into taking another 20 mg tablet of morphine. Frank was always a light sleeper easily awakened. I'm the opposite. When our children were babies and had late night and early morning feedings on demand, Frank had to wake me up. He'd give me a kiss and say, "Only an ultrasound sleeper wouldn't hear a baby crying loud enough to wake the dead."

The oxygen tank hissed and I checked that the tubes were still in Frank's nostrils. I couldn't let myself fall asleep or doze. I was lying in bed beside Frank with my head propped up on a pillow. We were alone together, a rolled up comforter between us so I wouldn't bump against his thin body, so we wouldn't even touch each other. I felt alone, but knew I wasn't. Did Frank feel alone, too?

I closed my eyes and prayed the Lord to stay awake.

Our Father who art in heaven, I began again, *hallowed be Thy name...* I saw my father sitting in his chair in the living room waiting for me, age fourteen, to go to our weekly religion class at St. Paul's Church so we could be confirmed as Anglicans. *Life* magazine was open on his lap. He turned the page and the paper rustled. He looked up, smiled, then winked at me, closed the magazine, and held it out to me.

I opened my eyes and, lit by a night light, I saw my father and Frank's father standing side by side at the foot of the bed, looking at me.

They were younger than we are.

My father Allan Blair died of a heart attack on Tuesday, November 9, 1948, at age 47. He would have been 48 on November 28. In the *Regina Leader-Post* editorial about his death titled "The Passing of a Great Healer" it said: "His wit was delightful, the twinkle in his eye constant. He had an underlying sense of humour that must have stood him in good stead in all his years of battling to make his dreams of cancer eradication come true."

Frank's father, Martin Krause, died of a heart attack on Tuesday, November 24, 1959, at age 63. In the family history book it says: "Martin was an outgoing, sociable person who loved sports, especially baseball, and dancing." There's a photograph of Martin and Frank's mother Elizabeth – Liz-kid to her daughters-in-law – that shows them in the same side by side old pals pose as my parents are in a wedding day snapshot. They're leaning toward each other, shoulders touching, each with an arm around the other.

Our fathers stood there, silently, Allan Blair and Martin Krause, who'd never met. I wanted to speak to them, but couldn't make my voice work. It was as if I was caught in one of those dreams that I know is a dream, but when I try to scream for help or run away from a killer with a knife, both my vocal cords and legs are paralyzed. The presence of our fathers gave me a strange feeling of comfort that everything was all right and, as they faded from sight, a stab of fear that I was just dreaming.

SUSTENANCE

The phone call from The China Doll restaurant the morning Frank's obituary appeared in the newspaper came as a complete surprise. A complimentary dinner would be delivered to my home if I let them know when to send it, the number of people it should serve, and what dishes I wanted. I was too stunned to ask whom I should thank for such an unusual act of kindness.

Later that day, Frank's brother Stan and I found out the Chinese food wasn't being paid for by his best friend Brownie, as we thought, but was being sent by the owner of the restaurant and his wife, Jimmy and Joanne Nikolou. That was another surprise. I hadn't seen either of them for years. When I phoned to say thank you, Jimmy told me that in the late 1960s when he was a new member of the Queen City Kinsmen and Joanne of Kinettes, Frank and I had asked them over to our house for drinks before their first Kinsmen dance and reserved a place for them at our table. He said what they'd dreaded going to had turned out to be a great welcome party, thanks to Frank's kinship.

On the first Saturday night after Frank's death, the day after his funeral, our dining room table and the buffet were laden with a sumptuous feast. Overwhelmed by life-and-death decisions, I'd let the restaurant select what dishes to send for twenty-five. There was enough food for twice that many to have second helpings.

Relatives and friends changed from sombre mourners to celebrants. Anecdotes were retold about young Frankie-*weisskopf*, Eyeball, husband, dad, grandpa, uncle, brother, brother-in-law, and best friend known as Mr. Air Canada. Puns, intended or not, were followed by the punster or someone else saying, "Frank would have liked that one."

It was a happy crowd. But that old forties wartime song kept going round and round in my mind about Saturday night being the loneliest night in the week. And I knew there'd be six other nights the same.

I broke open the fortune cookie I'd been holding and read the message: *Your home is a pleasant place from which you draw happiness.* Someday, I told myself, I'll make a list of why my house is a pleasant place thanks to the man of the house and I'll end it with my grocery list reminder to Frank: *Surprise for Pat!*

Ah yes, but it will begin with my surprise for Frank.

The thought makes me smile. It reminds me of how calm a good man can be when the woman he loves says, "Come and see what I did last night while you were in bed with your earphones on listening to hit tunes from the 1940s."

It surprised me that he liked my surprise. The proof is in the photos he took of me standing triumphantly between two of the studs I'd exposed with a hammer and screwdriver and broom handle crowbar prying off the wallboard. True, he didn't look pleased with the plasterboard scraps and drifts of dust at my feet. But knocking down a wall between two bedrooms we'd planned someday to join as our master bedroom and bath was a messy deconstruction job.

"Smile," Frank said, aiming the camera.

"No problem," I said. "This is the most satisfying non-sexual TGIF celebration I've ever had."

I took a couple of pictures of Frank doing his King Kong ape act hanging onto a stud. He was doing a growling Louis Armstrong rendition of "It's A Wonderful World."

And it was. Maybe still is – or will be again someday.

COMIC STRIP

Our son Jim phones reverse from the Victoria airport on his way home to Courtney after Frank's funeral, and says, all excited, "Dad's in good spirits. You're not going to believe this, Mom, but there's a coloured comic strip in the *Victoria Times Colonist* called *Frank And Ernest* that shows two guys named Frank and Ernest sitting at an anchor desk with a big sign on it that says *Eyeball News*. Frank reads the news and Ernest makes all sorts of Dad's kind of corny puns about it. What they're saying isn't in cartoon bubbles. What Frank and Ernest say is neatly printed in straight lines like Dad's labels on his tool box drawers and messages he left us kids on our to do lists of chores. Listen..."

He reads the six frames to me. We laugh and groan.

Later, Jim mails me a copy of the comic strip. There's an e-mail address on it I contacted, and after a couple of brief friendly exchanges of information, I'm a THAVES copyright assignee with permission to quote their Frank and Ernest on the Eyeball News in a memoir about my Frank Ernest Krause, nick-named Eyeball.

1.

FRANK: IN TONIGHT'S NEWS, A DOCTOR WITH A PHONY
DEGREE HAS TO PAY BACK ALL HIS FEES.

ERNEST: MOCK DOC IN HOCK!

2.

FRANK: IN OUR SCHOOLS THE NUMBER OF GOOD TEACHERS
IS DECLINING.

ERNEST: THERE'S A DESCENT IN DECENT DOCENTS!

3.

FRANK: A MONKEY BIT HIS OVERWEIGHT TRAINER AFTER THE
MAN STEPPED ON HIS FOOT.

ERNEST: CHIMP WITH LIMP PUTS CRIMP IN BLIMP!

4.

FRANK: STOP THAT, ERNIE! JUST FOR ONCE TRY TO BEHAVE
LIKE A PROFESSIONAL NEWSCASTER!

5.

FRANK: AND IN SPORTS, A SOCCER REFEREE WAS BEATEN UP
BY ROWDY FANS FROM THE UPPER LEVEL!

6.

ERNEST: ROOF RIFF-RAFF ROUGH REF!

As I keyboard it, I spend time laughing with the gods.

THE MOURNING NEWS BLUES

Woke up this morning a bleary-eyed widow alone in our double bed. Was I crying in my sleep? Frank died last week, two days before I turned sixty-five. He promised to be here to count the wrinkles in my birthday suit. He said, "If I'm the late love of your life by your big date, please wait on my side of our bed until I come back to celebrate." I crossed my heart and hoped to die if he did.

A sudden Greek salad attack last night made me unplug Frank's car, sweep off the snow, warm it up, and drive to the Lakeshore Restaurant for takeout with extra feta cheese and dressing and two slices of garlic toast. It was all done up in a white Styrofoam box and quilted aluminum foil like a belated birthday gift for me to take home to open and eat all alone with only his bewildered dog Scottie and TV to keep me company.

I watched O.J.'s case unfold without being told to switch the damn channel or turn down the sound so he wouldn't be disturbed by another bloody word while he read Donald Jack's book Me Too again one last time. He wasn't there in his La-Z-Boy chair to say that if he lived long enough – which he doubted – to just let him know when O.J. walked and was working on his golf score again.

Got up today with the breath of a goat. Stumbled to the vanity sink, fumbled for what I thought was our Scope mouthwash, unscrewed the top, tipped it up, took a sip to swish, and had the fuzz burned off my tongue and my mucous membrane stung by his Aqua Velva aftershave lotion.

Sputtering and spitting, my eyes watering like they do if I laugh so hard I cry, I see my Greek god in the vanity mirror lying on my side of the bed grinning at me. I hear him say, "Your

219

breath scorched my moustache and seared the stubble off my chin, but the good news is I don't have to get up to shave, and part of me is stirring to get up anyway so why don't you try to seduce me?"

I turn, looking coy, pretending I have to be coaxed, and realize I'm alone listening to a blues song I have no words to sing.

VACUUM

I am vacuuming in a vacuum today. My Electrolux man is absent. I need him. I am a vacuous vacuum cleaner. This has been his job for forty-four and a half years. We bought our first Electrolux before we were married in 1950, from the Saskatchewan manager of the company, Ab Coyne, a handsome man who could be mistaken for Gregory Peck. He and his exotically glamorous wife Audrey lived across the street from my family home on the east corner of Robinson and Hill Avenue. Their home was a newly built flat-roofed California bungalow with a ceiling to floor picture window the width of the house, facing the back alley. Their living room was like an outdoor movie screen for Sunday drivers who parked to watch a barefoot Ab wearing wildly striped satin lounging pyjamas, playing the grand piano, and Audrey, in one of the silky harem costumes she'd sewn, her waist-length auburn hair flowing and feet bare, dancing as temptingly as the love goddess Rita Hayworth did in the movie *Gilda*.

During my father's bedtime recovery from his next-to-last heart attack, Ab brought over copies of *Fortune* magazine for him to read and stayed up there in my parents' bedroom for long talkative visits punctuated by laughter. Sometimes they laughed so hard it rocked the house and the rest of the family would congregate in the bedroom to join in the fun. My father used to say, "Love and laughter make the world go round."

Ab may have been the Electrolux Man, but Frank was *my* Electrolux Man. I was the vacuuming observer after we were married and living in the heart of downtown Regina in the Grenfell Apartments. The living and sleeping room of our bachelor suite was small and the rug was postage stamp size, but the traffic on Hamilton Street was heavy so it got dusty and also linty from the bedclothes. Frank vacuumed at least once a week. This is the scene:

He puts on his cleaning outfit – the fedora he wants to get used to wearing before he ventures out in the business world in a hat, the honeymoon flannelette pyjamas he frequently takes off and folds before getting into bed with me, and his new leather slippers to break them in. The radio is on the hit parade station and "Goodnight, Irene" will be playing as soon as Louis Armstrong finishes singing "All Of Me," but the Murphy bed has to be up off the rug and we can't put it down until every last speck of dust is sucked off the carpet and the downtown-dirty Venetian blinds. Then, the first appliance we've ever bought, our sleek modern noisy Electrolux, has to be safely stowed away in its blanket before we lower the bed and strip tease. So here I am in my new high-heeled satin mules, my skin-tight gossamer bridal nightgown and bright Buchanan tartan dressing gown hiked up in a bunch over my knees, trying to do a slow sexy highland fling in the kitchen doorway. I know if I sing, "So why not take all of me..." my voice will be raspier than Louis's with desire. It might be beguiling enough to make my groom drop that damn Electrolux and take all of me right here on the terrazzo. I imagine undoing my dressing gown, shrugging it off my shoulders and letting it slide down my nightie to the floor. I shiver, and sing like a trumpet with a growler.

Where am I, now that I'm a new widow? I'm vacuuming in a master bedroom without a master. Our bed has been remade once by our middle daughter and five times by me since he died, but his clothes and his collection of ties are still neatly hung on his side of the closet. His polished shoes with shoetrees in them are placed on the shelf underneath. In the corner of our closet, almost hidden behind one of my shoe racks, those old 1950s genuine leather "Made In China" slippers of his are back where he left them with the wooden shoetrees in them. The soles bled reddish brown stains on the off-white carpet and the cleaners couldn't get his footprints out.

With the vacuum nozzle I take a swipe at the miniature venetians on the window beside the vanity of our master-less ensuite bedroom and the *shlumpf-shlumpf-snap-crack* sound of the blind's cord being sucked up is instant. I stub my big toe trying to hit the off switch with my foot fast enough to stop the motor before the cord tangles around the cylinder and strangles the choking roar. The blind is torn off the window and scrapes my ankles as it smacks down on my toes. I swear at the stupid Electrolux and yell at it that it isn't couth not to let me hear the satisfying *tings* of dirt and *shlumpfs* of fluff being sucked up its tube. But Frank's vacuum refuses to start and unwind the cord from its cylinder. The sound of silence is my toe throbbing. As I'm hopping across the room to sit down on Frank's side of the bed, I think of Miss Peggy Lee's torch song "Is That All There Is?"

I wish I could sing it, but I can't.

GONE AGAIN

I'm sitting on the kitchen bench Scottie sleeps under, facing the door to the carport, reading *The Globe And Mail* and rubbing Scottie's back with my stocking foot, a game he knows as "Socks," when something makes me look up. Scottie barks happily and runs to the door. Frank is standing there, smiling ear-to-ear at me. He's wearing a yarmulke. The tight white curls of his new growth of hair look like a halo that slipped down over the black prayer skullcap.

"For heaven's sake where on earth have you been?" I sound like my mother did fifty years ago when I was fifteen and she confronted me about coming home too late. But thank God I didn't ask, "Where in hell have you been?" (Editing and revising my questions and statements after I've spoken is a new habit.)

His smile and silence tell me to guess.

"A funeral at the synagogue?"

He keeps smiling.

Who died? What of? When? You shouldn't have gone without me.

He has on his black business suit, white shirt and red paisley tie that he was buried in. And no shoes. I sent them to the funeral home, but they were returned with a note to say footwear wasn't needed even for the viewing at prayers. Scottie nuzzles his bare feet. Frank doesn't look down. His smile begins to fade like the Cheshire cat's.

"Hey, wait." I stand up. "Better home late than never. I found the birthday card you bought me in the drawer of your bedside table. Very funny. It's a deal. I blow out the candles; you count the wrinkles in my birthday suit. It'll take you forever and a day."

I blink to clear my eyes and Frank's gone.

Scottie lies down, puts his nose at the crack under the door, and sniffs as if his nose is running.

Snow

After Frank was buried on that cold January day when tears froze as they were shed, I thought winter would never end. I felt as if I was driving alone in a blizzard, the curtain of snow endlessly parting yet never drawn open so I could see where I was going.

Each day seemed colder than the day before, the nights colder still. A lot colder. All I could do was try to read myself to sleep.

The poem I have on the fridge with the Air Canada maple leaf magnets on its corners is by Dave Margoshes:

> Rain always falls,
> snow is always cold,
> and the space we fill together
> has no more demands
> than when we're alone.

It was hard to remember that winter once brought excitement, that joy often came with freshly falling snow. Only by

225

concentrating long and hard, and searching through papers I haven't filed, was I able to find what I'd once thought about snow.

SNOW ANGELS

The first time I saw snow was in my birthplace of Tuscaloosa, Alabama, in January 1934 after I turned four years old. My transplanted mother, who had grown up in Indian Head, Saskatchewan, showed my black nursemaid Lily and me how to make angels in the sparkling white snow stars that covered the lawn. Our three angels were the only green grass showing in the front yards along University Boulevard for several hours. Lily bundled me up in extra layers of sweaters and wrapped us in a cocoon of blankets so we could sit awhile on the porch swing to contemplate our emerald angels lying on the white bed of snow as still as pinned butterflies.

"Lordy-Lord, see that sweet sight, honeychile?" Lily said. "Time comes we soar up to them golden gates in the great beyond, all God's children got the same colour soul."

"Green souls?" Mother smiled at Lily.

As we watched the snow around our green angels melt, Lily rocked the porch swing gently and sang "Amazing Grace." She ended with a verse that Mother said she'd never heard before. I thought it was a lullaby she made up for our angels.

BUMPER TAXI

In Frank's birthplace of Dysart, Saskatchewan, as soon as the roads were packed with snow, every car and truck that had a back bumper provided kids with a free ride to almost anywhere in town. On Saint's Day holidays and Sunday afternoons, Frank hitched bumper rides from his family's yellow clapboard house on Dysart's main street up the slight rise that everyone called The Hill to the cemetery. He would visit the side by side graves of an older sister and brother who died in March 1926, a year before he was born, and brush the snow off their granite stone crosses. Helen, age five and a half, and Ernest, age three, died of double pneumonia within one week of each other.

Young Frank Ernest, known as *Weisskopf* because of his mop of very light blond curly hair, was an expert bumper rider. He taught his little brother Stan how to hitch his hands on the bumper of a moving vehicle away from the exhaust pipe, crouch properly with his feet flat on the icy roadbed to slide smoothly, and let go at his destination without tumbling backwards heels over head or falling forward and getting ice-burns on his face.

All his life, Frank remembered exactly what he wore to bumper taxi. His feet were as warm as boiled perogies in two pairs of work socks and laced knee-high buckskin moccasins with felt insoles. He wore long grey underwear with a trap door, wool breeches, and a khaki First World War parka, all bought at the Army and Navy Surplus Store in far-off Regina. But the thick woollen mitts, scarves and toques he and Stan wore were multicoloured. Their mother and older sister Agnes hand-knit them using double strands of leftover scraps of wool sold for a nickel a bag at town rummage sales. Frank and Stan earned two pennies when they each held a skein of wool for his mom or sister to wind in a ball.

"Mom called us her Rainbow Boys," Frank said after he described what kept their heads, necks and hands warm outside in Dysart. "Times were tough. Stan and I had to wear all that stuff to bed in the ice-cold room Dad rented when we moved to Regina in the winter of '37. Dad let Mom keep the light bulb hanging from the ceiling on all night to get twenty-five watts of heat. Four in one bed didn't help much either. Stan and I agreed that it would have been warmer sleeping outside in a snow fort."

During an August heat wave in the seventies, Frank and I flew to Quebec City for a self-conducted immersion course in Canada's history. We came home with a winter scene of bumper riding that was once a rite of passage for boys, and some girls like me. The picture is hanging in a place of honour in our dining room.

We bought Print #37 of two-hundred of a street artist's etching titled: *Taxi bouttine*. The artist's signature is impossible to decipher. Bundled up in snowsuits of smudged-crayon colours that give them the worn look of hand-me-downs, three boys are ending their ride hanging on to the bumper of a late-forties Mercury. Frank and Stan laughingly referred to the third boy in the picture as Loopy Luke *Schinkenkopf,* and reminded each other that *Hamhead* always let go of the bumper at the wrong moment and somersaulted backwards on the road.

One day in November 1994, after he'd started radiotherapy, I caught Frank staring at the print as if he'd never seen it before. When he saw me watching him, he said, "It was a long way uphill to Dysart's cemetery and hard to let go."

BLIZZARD

The big blizzard of 1947 roared into Regina on Sunday, January 26, my seventeenth birthday. A handsome young man, who was going to be twenty years old on February 23, fought his way blindly through the whiteout to the snow castle on the edge of the prairie where I lived to bring me a solitaire pearl ring as a pledge of his undying love. He was plastered with snow from head to toe when he arrived.

My whole family was in the vestibule to see who'd braved the worst blizzard in living memory to ring our doorbell. He took off his snow-crusted black leather mitts and shook hands with my mother and father and kid brother Kenny.

My little sister Heather, age seven and an expert telephone eavesdropper, put her hands on her hips, and asked, "Why do the girls call you Eyeball?"

Frank showed her his glass eye trick.

"That's really neat," Heather said. "You could take it out and use it as a shooter when you play marbles. You'd never miss."

"A seeing-eye shooter," Frank said, rubbing his right eye. "Good idea."

We all laughed. I pinched Heather's shoulder.

Heather pinched me back on the hip, smiled up at Frank, and said, "My mother has invisible eyes in the back of her head that she only uses to spy on bad little girls."

It kept snowing and blowing full force for fourteen exciting days and nights after my birthday. Three days into the blizzard, the schools were closed and home deliveries of bread, milk and coal stopped.

Whole families joined together, linked to each other like a chain of fat snow people, to pull every available sled and toboggan, many of them homemade out of boxes on bobskates or skis or wooden skids, east to the last Lakeview stop on Albert Street to get essential supplies. Giant army trucks had been taken out of storage to haul bread, milk, and sacks of coal behind snowploughs to pickup sites on the outskirts. It looked as if the snouts of the trucks were attached to the blades of the ploughs as they crawled toward us or parked with their motors running. Heather nicknamed them "The Snow Dragons."

In those pre-balaclava days, the men who doled out what we needed wore brown paper bags over their heads. The bags were noosed around their necks with rope and had small eyeholes cut in them. "Bagmen," Heather called them.

Before the blizzard slowed down to intermittent snowstorms or just cold blustery days, the abandoned engine and twenty-seven cars of a freight train were buried on the Lewvan Line out near the airport under a snowdrift several miles long and forty feet high. When the location of the train was discovered, Stan was one of the grade twelve guys at Central who skipped ten days of classes to help dig it out for what was then the high wage of a dollar an hour.

A mile or so from the buried train over the new smooth white prairie foothills, a mountain of snow straddled two sides of our house at Hill Avenue and Robinson Street. The telephone pole at the end of our backyard looked like a short stump stuck in the snow. On the east side of our house, the leg of the mountain rose almost as high as the second-floor windows in the bedrooms of my parents and brother. My father decided to dig a tunnel through the mountain around to our back door.

It was a surgically precise procedure of planning and operation. First, he walked along the top of the mountain on snowshoes and probed its depth and stability with one of his ski poles held upside-down. Then, he drew maps and diagrams and charts of the tunnel on graph paper. Every last detail of the tunnel's design was shown: its length, width, depth; the curvature of the turn; how thick the roof would be; the arched shape of the openings; the calculated cubic feet of snow he would have to move elsewhere and the distance from the mouth of the tunnel to where the snow would have to be hauled.

I don't remember how long it took to complete the tunnel. Only one weekend, I think. My father's older brother, Uncle Wilf, and his son, my cousin Gordon, came down from their house a block away to help. Uncle Wilf was a dentist and knew how to excavate a cavity so the Blair brothers made a skilled tunnelling team. Everybody else helped carry and haul the blocks of snow away as the Doctor Blair brothers carved them out.

Just as my father had so carefully planned, the tunnel was eighteen feet long with a right turn west at the back gate, and then a roofless snow corridor to the igloo rotunda he'd designed and built with the best snow blocks at the back door. Only Heather could stand up perfectly straight to walk through the tunnel. The rest of us had to bend over just a little or quite a lot.

I have a snapshot of my father and me standing at the front entrance of the tunnel. He has his left arm around me and his right arm stretched out toward the camera. In his right hand, he's holding the spade that performed the artful snow surgery. After the picture was taken, he patted my shoulder with his left hand and thanked me for the good work I did as surgical nurse. Then he admired the architecture of his tunnel by saying, "Practising good medicine is art applied to science."

FROST

"Good King Wenceslas" isn't one of the carols on those endless instrumental tapes that shopping malls box our ears with so we'll pull out our plastic or cash and buy gifts. The good king's story needs lyrics.

As a child, I stood and listened to the story sung by Salvation Army quartets on downtown street corners, and I whispered the next words to sing to my brother and cousins during our annual Blair family circle singalong in front of our fireplace at home. A group of six of us in grade eight at Lakeview School named ourselves The Good Deed Girls Chorus and went door-to-door singing carols for donations to the children's Christmas fund. We always had more quarters dropped in our tin cup if the last carol we sang was about the good king who led the way and made footsteps in the snow for his page when they carried food, fuel and wine to a poor peasant.

Now, I rarely hear "Good King Wenceslas" sung or played on the radio, but when I do, it reminds me of the aftermath of our Krause clan Christmas dinner in 1962.

We took turns with Stan and his wife Guzz having the dinner and that year it was at the house they were renting on the 2000 block of Queen Street. There were four children in each family, pairs of cousins almost the same age from the two-year-olds to the girls age nine and ten. By late afternoon, the temperature had dropped to a Christmas day record of thirty-five below. It was unusual to hear the four oldest cousins discuss how cold it was and complain about all the clothes they had to wear even inside the house to keep warm. Frank and Stan warmed themselves up from the inside out at the kitchen bar. The rest of us were in the living room playing games and singing carols that focussed on winter weather. During our rendition of "Good King Wenceslas," Guzz led our visual and verbal illustration of the cold weather words.

When we sang, "the frost was cruel," we blew on our fingers, rubbed our toes, and covered our ears with our hands. The noises for "rude wind's wild lament" were interrupted by giggles and guffaws, and some soundless wind from cousins Marty and Jimmy that caused their older sisters to hold their noses. The words "bitter weather" were shown by choking and gagging, "the winter's rage" by raised fists, shadowboxing, foot stomping, kicking, and threatening words or gestures illustrated by crossed eyes.

When the fun and games ended, it was late, nearly nine o'clock, past bedtime for the children under ten. Frank came back in frozen stiff after starting the car and scraping the windows. Stan insisted on pouring him a warm-up nightcap and told Frank that after he'd downed it, he would get the flannelette pyjamas Guzz's mom sewed for him for Christmas to put on over his trousers. The children and I were standing at the door ready to go, and we were sweating bullets in so many layers of winter clothes. When I heard Frank agree Stan could top-up his nightcap, I took the kids out to rev the Chevy's motor.

The car was quite toasty by the time Frank came out wearing Stan's black balaclava and oversize red and white candy cane pyjamas over his parka and pants. He looked like Bozo the clown.

I locked my door on the driver's side. He tried to open it. I gestured to the passenger side and yelled, "I'm driving." He knocked on the window, pointed at the lock with one hand, and kept his other hand on the door handle. I roared the motor, honked the horn, and drew a semicircle around the front of the car to the passenger door. He walked to the front of the car and kept going straight south on Queen Street.

Judy, who'd moved over to the middle of the front seat and was almost sitting in my lap, said, "Where's Daddy going? Are we stuck?" From the back seat where he was wrapped in a blanket with his two younger sisters, Jimmy said, "He's making footsteps in the snow for us."

I shifted into gear and drove forward slowly behind Frank. He led us across Thirteenth Avenue, Fourteenth, and Fifteenth to Les Sherman Park where the road stopped, but he didn't. The snow was deep and crisp and even everywhere. Was he going to cross the creek? What if it was open under the snow? Would he make it to Seventeenth Avenue? Did I dare go see and take a chance of getting stuck driving down a quiet residential street with all my children in the car?

I drove home. Got the children settled in their beds. Studied a map at the kitchen table to figure out what route he might take to get here from there. Would he follow the curve of Coronation Street east to Argyle Road, come south again to Twenty-Fifth, turn east, cross Albert Street – that's always busy with speeding cars even when black ice patches make it dangerously slippery – walk to our corner, turn south and come home? Home where the heart is – and the tongue-lash. I was so scared I felt as if I was going to be sick to my stomach.

I went upstairs to our bedroom, turned out the light, and stood at our bedroom window to watch. And pray. I stood there watching for him forever.

And when he appeared, as soon as I was sure it was him walking south from our corner, I stripped down to my long thermal underwear, put my flannelette nightgown on over it, kicked off my shoes, climbed into bed as close to the edge of my side as I could without falling out, pulled up the comforter, shut my eyes and pretended to be sound asleep.

Brightly shone the moon that night when he finally got into bed beside me and snuggled up to me. I didn't stir.

The frost was cruel.

ROLLERS

On Christmas Eve morning, 1993, invisible angels danced across our white feather tick lawn rolling up pillowy snowballs to build themselves partners. Frank and I knelt side by side on the loveseat in front of the living room window, elbows resting on the back, chins cupped in our hands to keep our mouths from hanging open, mesmerized by the magic performance. We watched the whirl of angels waltz and polka, jitterbug and swing in a blur of snowy white wings.

Frank said, "I like the constant surprises of prairie winters. The hip-hip-hurrahs of nature's extremes."

After the angels vanished and abandoned parts of their partially rolled-up snow partners were scattered on the snow slowly melting out of shape in the sun, I felt scared. I tried not to see pillowing lymph nodes in Frank's bone marrow, rolling up his spinal column to his brain, strangling the breath from his lungs, bulging out of his armpits and abdomen and groin. When I shut my eyes, I didn't want to see hordes of malignant black snow angels with spiked wings inside him batting iced snowballs that grew larger and larger rolling through his blood and the chemical sludge in his collapsing veins.

Later, on the TV suppertime news, we found out there was an official weather name for the free rolling snowballs that graced every open stretch of new fallen snow in Regina for almost two hours. Environment Canada called them "snow rollers." Not "holy rollers," which, for one hopeful moment, I believed I'd heard. I imagined a heaven-sent cleansing, cancerous lymph nodes dissolving, rolling away like clouds, melting to nothing on a sunshiny day.

And I prayed for the spontaneous remission of Frank's cancer that the specialists call: *a whisper of nature.*

THE SNOWBIRDS

On December 22, 1994, we had one of those mild melting afternoons of hoarfrost and sun-splashed snow that turn Regina into a winter wonderland. I put on the red parka Frank gave me on a Valentine's Day in another life, before we knew that each change of season could be our last, and went out to build a snow couple in front of the living room windows where we could see them from our chairs.

The stickiness of the snow was perfect.

For the bases, I packed snow around two mounds of frozen earth Frank had dumped from the big clay pots that all summer held geraniums with giant red pompom blooms. As I rolled up the abdomens and heads for the snow couple, drivers honked, neighbours offered to help me lift them in place, and some kids walking by to school gave me a thumbs-up and said, "Cool."

After Frank awoke from a long nap in his recliner, we rummaged through the kind of stuff kept by people who've lived in the same house for forty years. Laughing at our memory mirages, we chose items to turn the snow couple into a pair of snowbirds in Florida.

For her: my 1960s black-as-a-crow's-wing hairpiece as bangs; a once snazzy red straw sunhat; my rose-coloured sunglasses that our youngest daughter secretly wore in her early teens until a boy said the humongous round lens made her look like a housefly with pink eye; a brass button off Frank's old TCA blazer to symbolize the cute snub nose I'd longed for in high school – before I found out it was because Frank had admired my "patrician profile" in the Detention Room that he asked me out; and smiling red pepper lips that didn't run crinkly lipstick rivulets into the snow around them.

For him: the red and blue Budweiser porkpie hat Frank bought at the first Florida spring training ball game we went to; "Great Flying Ace" aviator glasses our son wore night and day after graduating to a two-wheel bike; one of the pair of fake noses and attached moustaches Frank and I wore to a 1950s Halloween party disguised as Siamese twins; and a wide lopsided cranberry-chain smile.

For both: tied around their shoulders so the red maple leaf logo showed, Air Canada beach towels Frank won in a long-ago sales promotion for snowbird flights.

Tomorrow, we said, we'll take pictures of the happy couple standing side by side on our snow-white beach and use the best one on our season's greeting card next year.

That winter solstice night, the snowbirds were smashed. Only their bases of frozen earth sat upright. Hair, hats, glasses, and torn pieces of their red costumes were scattered near them. We hoped whoever kicked them apart bruised their toes.

When I tried to put the snowbirds together again the snow was too sugary. I struggled not to cry.

THE SNOWMAN

A week to the day after Frank died, Tuesday, January 31, I opened the venetian blinds in the living room, and a snowman with wide-open twig arms was standing beside the snowbird bases with his back to me. I put my parka on over my dressing gown, pulled on my boots, and went out to see what he looked like. He had charcoal pellet eyes, a carrot nose, smiling red apple-peel lips, and on his head he was wearing a jaunty orange plastic Kash & Karry visor tipped sideways over one eye.

There were no signs anywhere of snow being rolled up to build him. The photographs our niece Jackie came over and took that morning show that's true.

Many times Frank and I had told the story of the snowbirds being built and smashed on winter solstice. Friends, relatives, and neighbours heard it over Frank's last holiday season.

People who came to visit after Frank died listened to me tell the snow couple story by myself and reacted with sadness mixed with anger at the senseless vandalism.

Then I told them the sequel about how the handsome snowman outside the window had appeared out of nowhere seven days after Frank died and landed where the snowbirds were. I asked a lot of people if they'd built him.

My writer friends said no, but they wished they'd dreamed up such a good idea. The neighbours all said they hadn't heard or seen anything suspicious that night.

Frank's airline buddies agreed the snowman flew in on an Air Canada pass. Using Frank's thirty-three-year priority, one of them added, and his photo ID in a shirt and tie.

I'm A-okay with that theory, I said.

Life is full of many wonderful mysteries. I accepted the solution to the snowman's origin as magic. And, when spring came and the snow melted, I could see the ghost of my snowman guarding the patch of orange Iceland poppies.

Three quotes about living and dying comfort me.

Fats Waller's one-liner: "One never knows, do one?"

Lines from Sister Mary Madeleva's "Knights-Errant":

> Death is no foeman, we were born together;
> He dwells between the places of my breath.

Night vigil at my heart he keeps and whether
I sleep or no, he never slumbereth.

And three lifelines from "Late Song" by poet Gwendolyn
MacEwen who gave her poems a pulse. It's *our* poem:

But it is never over; nothing ends until we want it to.
Look, in shattered midnights,
On black ice under silver trees, we are still dancing, dancing.

These things and more are cures for sorrow.

Acknowledgments

I t was lucky that my apprenticeship to be a published author
began in Saskatchewan where experienced writers offer begin-
ners a lot of help. Thanks to my first 1970s mentors, Ken
Mitchell, Jean Freeman, Bob Currie and Mossie Hancock, I had
an exciting start.

For six years, I co-ordinated and participated in the writing
workshops at the former Saskatchewan Summer School of the
Arts at Fort San and worked on a fiction manuscript. The students and instructors were enthusiastic, energetic, creative crit-
ics and inspired editors. I was one of many happy writers whose
first book was published after it was workshopped at Fort San
and won a major Saskatchewan award in manuscript.

Now, in 2007, I'm grateful for literary organizations and services writers helped establish: the Saskatchewan Arts Board assistance programs; the Saskatchewan Writers Guild (SWG); *Grain*
magazine; writing retreats; literary presses like Coteau Books;
competitions and readings; City of Regina Arts Commission
writer's grant; the annual Book Awards; Sage Hill Writing
Experience; Gary Hyland's Moose Jaw Festival of Words; and my
friends at the Regina Public Library Telephone Information

Services who can find out that *Slesse* is Salish for *fang*. Plus, I'm very lucky to have had the good-natured, patient and creative editor Bob Currie work with me again as he did for my second book of short stories, *Best Kept Secrets* (Coteau Books 1988).

Thanks to Ven Begamudré for advice on reverse story structure; Amy Nelson-Mile for urging me to enter the Hicks competition; Gordon Grice, author of *The Red Hourglass* that begins with my father's black widow spider experiment.

And a very special thanks to my writing group: Byrna Barclay, Brenda Niskala, Bob Currie and Dave Margoshes.

Acknowledgements

HONEY HUSH
Words by Ed Kirkeby Music by Thomas "Fats" Waller
© Copyright 1939 by Bourne Co. and OTHER PUBLISHER
Copyright Renewed
All Rights Reserved. International Copyright Secured

The selected lines of poetry by Sister Mary Madeleva are reprinted with the permission of Sister Joy O'Grady, President of the Congregation of Sisters of the Holy Cross.

The Thomas Lynch description that "mourning is a romance in reverse," from his book *The Undertaking – Life Studies from the Dismal Trade*, is reprinted with the permission of W. W. Norton & Company, Inc.

The Joel Vance quotes from his biography *Fats Waller: His Life and Times*, are reprinted with the permission of Jeremy Robson, Chrysalis Books Co. UK.

Selected lines from "Late Song" by Gwendolyn MacEwen (*Afterworlds*, McClelland & Stewart, 1987) are reprinted with permission granted by the author's family.

The C.S. Lewis quotation, from his book *A Grief Observed*, is reprinted with the permission of the C.S. Lewis Company Limited.

Nashville Hall of Fame songwriter, singer, whistler and bandleader Carson J. Robison [1890-1959] wrote both the music and words for more than 200 songs. In 1932, Robinson and his band, The Buckaroos, performed in England for King George and Queen Elizabeth. "The Wreck of the Number Nine" is one of the first songs he wrote in the late 1920s and RCA Victor recorded. The lyrics are reprinted with the permission of his family.

The dialogue of the coloured comic strip FRANK & ERNEST EYEBALL NEWS is reprinted by agreement with UNITED MEDIA, Newspaper Enterprise Association.

About the Author

Pat Krause has two previous book publications, the short story collections *Best Kept Secrets* and *Freshie*. She is an award-winning writer of fiction and non-fiction and was for many years a writer/commentator for CBC Radio in Regina. She also worked as communications officer at the University of Regina, as the administrator of a medical tape library for doctors, and as a part-time apartment-rental agent.

Pat Krause was born in Tuscaloosa, Alabama, where her father, Dr. Allan Blair, was on the medical faculty of the University of Alabama. When her family returned to Canada in 1934, they lived in Winnipeg, Indian Head, Toronto, and, in 1939, moved to her father's hometown of Regina, where he became internationally known as director of Sasatchewan's advanced cancer treatment services. The Allan Blair Cancer Centre in Regina was named in his honour after his death in 1948. Pat continues to make her home in Regina.